QUEST

COMPANION 3

Y5/p6

SARAH FLEMING

Contents

UNIT 1

Read Bertie's Survival Manual: How to Encounter the World's Most Dangerous Animals and Live to Tell the Tale. It might just save your life!

● Narrative, poems and recount

Uncle Bertie's Wacky Survival Manual *by Errol Lloyd* **4**

Chapter one 4

Chapter two 5

Chapter three 6

Chapter four 7

Chapter five 8

Chapter six 11

Chapter seven 12

Chapter eight 14

Chapter nine 16

UNIT 2

● Recounts

Welcome to my world!

Earth Speaking: My Life – Some Highlights **18**

Introduction 18

My life 20

Time for some science 22

Different types of plate movements 24

Back to my life story 26

An evolutionary case history – marsupials 28

An evolutionary case history – islands 30

Back to Bali 32

Glossary 33

UNIT 3

The 20th century shaped the car and the car shaped the 20th century. Drive on to find out how.

● Reports and explanations

THE CENTURY OF THE CAR **34**
by Steve New

Introduction 34

War 36

Safety 38

Car power 38

Speed 40

Mass production and computers 42

Special cars 44

Fictional cars 46

The future of the car 47

The Car Trip
by Michael Rosen 48

UNIT 4

Let there be light! Find out how different cultures explain where the sun came from.

● Myths, narrative poetry

Here Comes the Sun — 50

Introduction 50

Sun myth from Canada: The Crow Brings the Daylight 50

Sun myth from Australia: The Kookaburra and the Sun 55

Sun myth from Greece: The Twins: Sun and Moon 59

Hiawatha's Childhood *by Longfellow* 62

UNIT 5

Where might your nose hairs freeze? What's the 'White City'? What did an elephant bird look like?

● Leaflets to persuade

Travel Trivia — 64

Introduction 64

Algeria 66

Guatemala 68

Japan 70

Madagascar 72

Monaco 74

Russia 76

UNIT 6

There are hundreds of castles in the United Kingdom. Welcome to four of them.

● Reports, stories from other cultures

A Kingdom of Castles — 78

Introduction 78

Motte and bailey castles 78

Cardiff Castle, South Glamorgan, Wales 79

The Legend of King Arthur *by Roger Lancelyn Green* 80

Dunluce Castle, County Antrim, Northern Ireland 82

The Legend of Finn MacCool and the Giant's Causeway *retold by Kate Ruttle* 84

Balmoral Castle, Aberdeenshire, Scotland 87

Dover Castle, Kent, England 92

Castle glossary 93

INDEX 94

Uncle Bertie's
Wacky Survival Manual

by Errol Lloyd

Chapter one

Uncle Bertie was a show-off. Once, he unbuttoned his shirt and showed me some scars on his chest.

'I got this fighting a lion in Africa,' he boasted.

I thought he was fibbing. 'Was it a circus lion?' I teased.

'Circus!' he bellowed. 'Are you kidding? It was a wild lion with a shaggy mane and real, sharp claws. None of this pretend circus stuff.'

'And what happened, Uncle? Did you manage to run away?'

'Me? Run away? Never! I killed the beast with one thrust of my dagger. It fell dead at my feet.'

Next, he rolled up his left shirt sleeve to reveal four big scars. 'Do you know where I got these?'

'No,' I said. But before he could tell me, Mum intervened. 'Ashley, have you done your homework?'

I hadn't, and she sent me to my room.

'I'll tell you some other time,' said Uncle Bertie, winking at me.

Chapter two

But I didn't get to find out, as the next time I saw him, Uncle Bertie was waving us off at the airport. My parents had got jobs teaching at a school in a remote East African village where we were to live for a year. I wasn't crazy about the plan as I was sure I'd miss London and my friends.

As we left for the departure lounge, Uncle Bertie thrust a booklet in my hand titled, 'BERTIE'S SURVIVAL MANUAL'. It was in his own handwriting and had a subtitle, 'How to Encounter the World's Most Dangerous Animals and Live to Tell the Tale'.

'You'll need to read every word of this,' he said. 'Trust me!'

I promised I would read it on the plane, but instead I watched a kung fu movie. After that, I was too tired for reading, so I put Uncle Bertie's manual away and slept for the rest of the flight.

How to escape from stampeding elephants without a scratch!

Elephants travel in groups of 30 to 50 animals, so when they stampede, there's a lot of them!

Use your ears. If you hear a great thundering of earth, a crashing of trees and a shrill trumpeting, it's time to take action! But, however scared you are, DON'T turn and run from a stampeding elephant. Instead, stand your ground and clap your hands. I also recommend saying loudly and clearly (but not shouting), 'And stop there, you great lump.'

It'll stop the elephants in their tracks every time.

Chapter three

The village in Africa was a mixture of traditional mud-walled houses and modern concrete ones, around a central courtyard. The African landscape seemed gigantic and endless. We could scan the horizon and hardly see any sign of human life. All we saw were rolling savannahs inhabited by lots of wildlife (as I was about to discover).

I read all the books in the school library (there weren't many). After I had read them all I just made up my own stories in my head – adventure stories full of fierce African animals and strange sights and sounds. Sometimes the days were so hot and languid that I couldn't tell whether I was really awake and doing things or just daydreaming.

I guess it was out of boredom that I turned to Uncle Bertie's manual. I found that it had all kinds of weird and wonderful facts about dangerous animals. I often laughed aloud as I read, but little did I know that this wacky handbook was to save my life on more than one occasion during the coming year.

The African savannah is like a huge grass meadow, covered with trees and shrubs. There is a dry season and a rainy season. Lots of different animals and birds live there. Some of the animals, like lions, are hunters, while others, like gazelles, are the prey.

Chapter four

I had been told a hundred times not to go off wandering by myself in the African bush, but I didn't take much notice.

My first scare, big time, came one Saturday when Mum and Dad were visiting the local market, and I stopped reading Uncle Bertie's manual to go exploring on my own. Suddenly, I came face to face with a huge lion. He had rippling muscles and fierce eyes that fixed on mine.

My first instinct was to run, but, thank goodness, I remembered Uncle Bertie's manual which warned that running away is an attack trigger to a lion, and that lions can run much faster than humans.

But what was I to do? Again, the manual came to my rescue: 'Stare them in the eyes and don't look away.'

I forced myself to stare the lion down, even though my legs had turned to jelly. The lion growled and bared his teeth and crouched for an attack.

I shouted, 'Get lost, you ugly brute!' which were the exact words the manual recommended if all else failed. It worked. My shouts broke the lion's concentration. He turned and scampered off. I ran all the way back home.

The Lion

If you're attacked by a Lion
Find fresh underpants to try on
Lay on the ground quite still
Pretend you are very ill
Keep like that day after day
Perhaps the lion will go away

Spike Milligan

Chapter five

After that, I only went out in the company of Jomo, our gardener. He knew all about survival skills in the African bush. He taught me how to make fire without matches, how to track animals and how to find water and stuff to eat. He confessed to me that, in his younger days, he had been a poacher, until he reformed and became a tourist safari guide. In the off season, he worked as a gardener.

One day, Jomo took me across the nearby river in his dug-out canoe to the plot of land he cultivated. Whilst he was busy at work, I browsed through Uncle Bertie's manual which I now carried around in my pocket wherever I went. On a wild impulse, I decided to sneak a spin in Jomo's canoe. In midstream I accidentally hit a hippopotamus with the paddle. The hippo got mad and attacked the canoe,

Truth or tall tale?
Lion

Lions are Africa's largest carnivores. They can run at speeds of up to 80 kph – a lot faster than a human being. Lions usually stay with other members of their pride, sleeping by day and hunting at night. They do not like loud noise or fire.

But do you think Ashley is telling the truth about meeting a lion? To meet a single lion during the day would be unusual.

Uncle Bertie's manual is right this time. In the unlikely event of meeting a lion, the best way of avoiding being attacked would be to back away, or to make a lot of noise and try and scare it.

Lion, The

The Lion, the Lion, he dwells in the Waste,
He has a big head and a very small waist;
But his shoulders are stark, and his jaws
   they are grim,
And a good little child will not play with him.

Hilaire Belloc

hurling me into the water. Uncle Bertie's manual warned that hippos, weighing as much as four tons, have a mouth span of up to 1.2 metres wide and can swallow you in one go! I swam frantically towards the riverbank. I wasn't far from safety when I spotted a giant crocodile craftily slinking into the water. All I could see after that was the tip of the reptile's nose and eyes sticking out of the water as it glided menacingly towards me.

Suddenly, the croc dived and I braced myself for an attack. I grabbed a bit of stick floating by to poke him in the eye as suggested in the manual.

The Hippopotamus

Behold the hippopotamus!
We laugh at how he looks to us,
And yet in moments dank and grim,
I wonder how we look to him.
Peace, peace, thou hippopotamus!
We really look all right to us,
As you no doubt delight the eye
Of other hippopotami.

Ogden Nash

Truth or tall tale?
Hippopotamus

Hippos have been known to attack canoes when defending their territory. They can weigh up to 4500 kg, and their tusks can be over 1.5 m long. Hippos can kill people by delivering a powerful bite. However, they are strict vegetarians, feeding on grass and water plants.

So hippos would not swallow a person whole as Bertie's manual says. Ashley could be telling the truth in this case. Do you believe him?

9

The croc surfaced and lunged towards me with its mouth wide open, revealing a scary set of jagged teeth. Without thinking, I thrust out my hand with the stick held vertically and, in an instant, jammed the croc's mouth open. He swam round and round shaking his head wildly, but the stick held firm. Using the stick in that way wasn't in the manual, but it worked a treat!

Amazingly there was no damage to the canoe. On the way home, I pleaded with Jomo not to tell my parents, promising that I would keep out of trouble in future.

The Crocodile

How doth the little crocodile
Improve his shining tail,
And pour the waters of the Nile
On every golden scale!

How cheerfully he seems to grin,
How neatly spreads his claws,
And welcomes little fishes in,
With gently shining jaws!

Lewis Carroll

Truth or tall tale?
Crocodile

Because crocodiles' eyes are sensitive and vital to help them hunt, crocodiles will let go of prey if their eyes are threatened.

Crocodiles have between 64 and 70 teeth, which are always growing. They use their razor-sharp teeth for catching and holding their prey. They also have very powerful jaws. The upper jaw is all bone and is not very flexible, but the lower jaw is very loose and flexible.

So Uncle Bertie's advice about crocs' eyes would be very helpful! But about the mouth … this means that a crocodile's jaws are very strong and can open very wide, so Ashley's stick would have had to be very strong and just the right length too.

Chapter six

I kept my promise to Jomo, but sometimes trouble comes looking for you – this time in the shape of a scorpion.

One night, I had fallen asleep reading Uncle Bertie's manual when, in the middle of the night, the creepy-crawly crept into my room, crawled into my left shoe and snuggled up for the night. The next morning, I woke up and got dressed. The last thing I did was to put on my shoes before setting out on the three-kilometre trek to school.

I had been walking for about five minutes when I felt a terrific pain in my left big toe. I yelled and yanked off the shoe. The scorpion fell to the ground and scurried away into the bushes.

I was convinced that I was going to die – as much from the pain as from the venom. I hobbled to school but by the time I got there the pain had died down. Scorpions weren't mentioned in Uncle Bertie's manual, but I later learned that their bites are seldom fatal. Just the same, after that, each night before I went to bed, I locked my shoes safely away in a cupboard.

The Scorpion

The scorpion is as black as soot,
He dearly loves to bite;
He is a most unpleasant brute
To find in bed at night.

Hilaire Belloc

Truth or tall tale?
Scorpion

Scorpions use their venom to capture and kill prey and to defend themselves. Despite their bad reputation, few types of scorpions have venom strong enough to kill humans. Most people who are stung by scorpions are stung on the foot. Often this happens at night, when they don't have shoes on, or when scorpions have crawled into their shoes.

Sometimes, scorpions can deliver a 'dry' sting which doesn't have any venom in it. The victim can show false signs and symptoms of a venomous sting through sheer panic.

So, Ashley was right to lock his shoes away. But is it possible that brave Ashley might just have been panicking about the sting in the first place …?

Chapter seven

My scare with the giant croc and then the scorpion made me especially interested in arachnids and reptiles. Uncle Bertie's manual was really hot on snakes. It warned that some of the world's more venomous snakes live in Africa and that I should avoid them like the plague. Top of the list was the black mamba, which had enough venom to kill you within an hour if you couldn't get a shot of anti-venom in time.

One day, with the manual safely tucked away in my pocket, I went off on a field trip in search of small reptiles. I found a rocky area and busied myself turning over stones, peeping into crevices and just sort of poking around. What I had in mind were lizards and salamanders and small harmless snakes, but what I got was quite different.

It really started when I was feeling so hot and thirsty that I found a shady tree to rest under, take a sip of water from my hip flask and eat my packed lunch. Afterwards, I relaxed in the shade of the tree and read the last chapter on reptiles in Uncle Bertie's manual. Eventually I felt drowsy, and I put the manual in my pocket and fell asleep.

Big mistake. Never fall asleep when reptiles are around. What I had forgotten was that snakes live not just under rocks, but in trees as well. I remember I woke from my slumber and, by chance, I looked up and found myself staring straight into the big, pitiless eyes of a coal black, two-metre-long, black mamba.

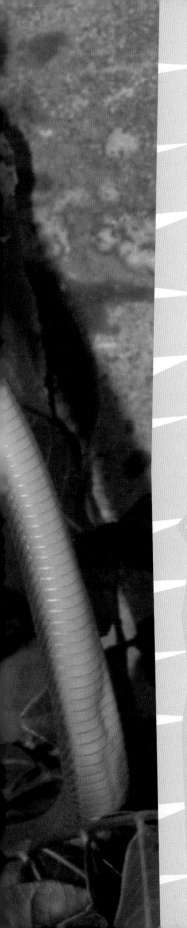

I should have put as much distance between myself and the mamba as I could, but I remember being mesmerised by how big its eyes were in such a small head. All I could think was that the snake was saying to me, 'All the better to see you with!'

In a panic I got up to run. The black mamba, without a moment's hesitation, struck out at me. It must have been aiming for my thigh, for it bit straight into the manual which, luckily, was in my hip pocket.

Uncle Bertie's manual had saved my life. By some strange coincidence the snake had bitten straight through to the section on reptiles and deposited its venom on page 17 which featured black mambas.

After that, I was really proud of my manual and showed the snake's toothmarks to my parents, to Jomo, to all my schoolfriends and just about anybody who would listen to my story.

Just the same, I took it as a warning and kept well away from trees in rocky areas after that.

Truth or tall tale?
Black mamba

Black mamba snakes are the fastest land snakes in the world. They can reach top speeds of 16-20 kph in short bursts over level ground.

Hmm, so did Ashley know about black mambas not being black?

Despite their name, black mambas aren't black – they're grey. The name comes from the colour inside the snake's mouth – something it will gladly show you if you threaten it!

Black mambas can grow to 4.3 m long and are one of the most poisonous snakes in the world, as just two drops of their venom will kill a human.

13

Chapter eight

When our time in Africa was coming to an end, I complained to Jomo that I didn't have any photos of wild animals to show to my mates when I returned home. Jomo borrowed a safari jeep and took me to the game reserve park.

From the safety of the jeep I took pictures of wild buffalo, a pack of hyenas scavenging a dead wildebeest, a leopard and her cub and loads of other animals. We stopped for a picnic and Jomo disappeared to fetch some wood to light a fire for a barbecue.

Suddenly, a herd of black rhinoceros appeared in the distance. I knew from Uncle's manual that rhinos have poor eyesight, so I thought I'd creep up on them and get some cool close-up pictures.

I remembered, too, that they had a keen sense of smell, so I licked my finger and held it up to check the direction of the wind before approaching them.

The Rhinoceros

The rhino is a homely beast,
For human eyes he's not a feast,
But you and I will never know
Why nature chose to make him so.
Farewell, farewell you old rhinoceros
I'll stare at something less prepoceros.

Ogden Nash

When I was within 50 metres of the herd I started to take shots of a mother rhino and her baby calf. I forgot that they have sharp hearing and they must have heard the clicking of the camera, for the next thing I knew, the mother was charging me at full speed with her horn stuck out like the business end of a battle tank.

I started to run, but I stubbed my toe and stumbled. I could feel the earth shaking as the rhino closed in on me. I could never have made it back to the jeep in time, so I quickly scampered up to the top of the nearest tree.

I thought I was safe until the rhino headbutted the tree and dislodged me from the branch I was clinging to. As I fell, I managed to grab hold of a lower branch. The rhino was circling for another charge when Jomo came to my rescue. He drove the jeep towards the baby rhino, blaring the horn. The mother then turned and chased the jeep instead. Jomo cleverly drove off, away from the tree.

Later, when things had died down, Jomo drove back, collected me and dressed my bleeding big toe.

He didn't speak to me all the way home.

Truth or tall tale?
Rhinoceros

Rhinoceroses have extremely poor vision, but a good sense of smell. When they are threatened, rhinoceroses sometimes charge towards the scent or sound that is upsetting them.

Uncle Bertie's manual is right about rhinos having poor eyesight and a good sense of smell. Although rhinos are strong and heavy, is it likely that one could have knocked Ashley from the tree?

The **smallest** rhinoceros (the Sumatran) reaches a shoulder height of about 1.2 m and weighs about 1000 kg. The **largest** rhinoceros (the white rhino) can reach a shoulder height of up to 1.85 m and weigh more than 3000 kg.

Chapter nine

By the time I said goodbye to Jomo we were firm friends again, and he gave me a wooden carving of a little grass snake as a farewell present.

Back in London, Uncle Bertie met us at the airport and drove us home. Whilst my parents were upstairs unpacking, he asked me if I had found his survival manual useful.

I told him about my exploits with the lion, the hippo, the giant croc, the black mamba and the rhino.

While telling him about the black mamba, I proudly showed him the toothmarks in the manual. I know I shouldn't have done it, but I had used a nail to increase the size of the toothmarks so that they

were now quite a bit bigger and reached as far as page 42 on king cobras. It was just a little fib, but it made the story a lot more interesting.

Uncle wasn't as impressed as I thought he'd be.

'But have you got any scars to show?' he asked, rolling up his shirt sleeve again to show the four scars I know he must have been itching to tell me about for a whole year.

Scars! At the time of the attacks I was glad to have got away unscathed, but now I really wished I had even one scratch to show off like a trophy.

Then I had a touch of inspiration.

'There's just one small scar I have, Uncle,' I said. I took off my shoes and socks and held up my left big toe for inspection.

'There,' I said, pointing to where I had stubbed my big toe running away from the rhino.

'How did you get that?' he asked.

'I was attacked by this gigantic scorpion,' I said. 'He was as big as a lobster. He grabbed me by the big toe and wouldn't let go. In the end I gave him a karate chop and he ran away into the bushes. I saved my own life by sucking out the poison.'

Uncle Bertie seemed impressed and nodded approvingly.

'Now, about these four scars,' he said, pointing to his arm. 'Have you ever been locked in mortal combat with a great white shark?'

Sharks were not in his survival manual. He must have a whole new chapter on the world's most dangerous sea creatures to add to the manual, I thought.

I braced myself for some tall tales that would probably stretch well into the night when, once again, Mum intervened.

'I suppose, Bertie, he's been telling you about the time a grass snake bit your survival manual?' she said.

'And the lion and the giant crocodile and the …' began Uncle Bertie.

'Honestly,' she interrupted, wagging her finger at me. 'I don't know which one of you is a bigger fibber, you or your uncle.'

I *knew* Ashley was fibbing in bits of the story! Did you?

Unit 2

My Life – Some Highlights

I'm Earth, your host for this unit. First, a little puzzler.

ASIA · **INDONESIA** · **PAPUA NEW GUINEA** · Java · **AUSTRALIA**

THE PLACE: Indonesia THE TIME: now

See those islands, curving from Java towards Papua New Guinea?

They look like beads on a necklace, all on the same string, right? **Wrong.**

See the islands called Bali and Lombok? They're only 25 km apart.

What if I told you that these islands started life on opposite sides of the Earth from each other?

Crazy, but true.

Java · Bali · Lombok

One of the ways you can tell is by looking at their wildlife. Although the islands are next to each other, the wildlife you find on them is very different.

 There is a glossary of words about me on page 33 which you might find helpful in this unit.

Lombok (and all the islands EAST of it) has the kinds of animals you find in Australia.

Cockatoo

tiger

Bali (and all the islands WEST of it) has the kinds of animals you find in Asian countries.

 That would be like having giraffes and flamingos living in France, and only boring rabbits and pigeons living in England, only 34 km across the English Channel.

To find out why, we have to start before I was born ...

My life

1 This is a picture of my parent, the Sun, when it was just a baby. The Sun was born 5 billion years ago – only 8 billion years after the Big Bang, when the whole universe was created! When the Sun was finished, it was a medium-bright star, and there was a cloudy disc of leftover gas and dust swirling round it.

2 This is a close-up of part of that cloudy disc around the Sun. The cloudy stuff is what I'm made of – lots of dust swirling around. This picture shows bits clumping together to make me. Lots and lots of bits bumped into each other and stuck together, and I grew and grew until finally ...

3 I was born 4600 million years ago. Cool! I was hot stuff when I was young – red hot, molten and fuming.

4 That's me! By the time I was 600 million years old, I'd settled down enough to form a crust on my surface – not everywhere, mind you. I still enjoyed the odd volcano party! I was a right raver and wow – did I pong!

 20

The gases I let rip hung around near my surface and made an atmosphere. I've got a great atmosphere now, but way back then I was pretty poisonous. As I got older, I calmed down and cooled off a bit and got my first taste of RAIN!

5 Well, with enough rain, I ended up with oceans.

And then – about 3600 million years ago – life began. In a small way, admittedly, but having life makes me a VERY SPECIAL planet.

Tiny life form

13 billion years ago
Big Bang
The universe begins.

5 billion years ago
The birth of the Sun
The Sun is formed from bits of an older star that exploded.

4.6 billion years ago
The birth of Earth
The Earth is formed from bits left over from the Sun.

3.6 billion years ago
Life on Earth
Simple and very tiny forms of life appear.

OK, now a bit of science. My surface cooled down, but I'm still hot inside – so hot that even rock goes gooey. This gooey rock is my magma, and it flows around me very slowly.

My surface cooled into about 15 big bits – tectonic plates they're called, with edges that join together like a jigsaw puzzle. Imagine a jigsaw puzzle on the surface of a ball – that's what my plates are like.

Only I am no ordinary spherical jigsaw – no – because my plates *move and change shape.*

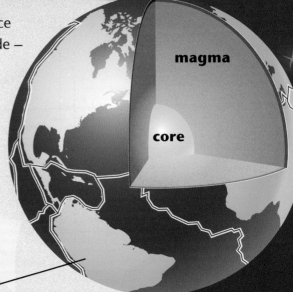

magma

core

tectonic plates

Cutaway of the Earth showing tectonic plates as they are today.

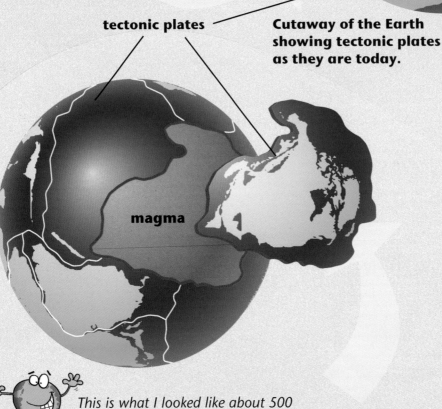

magma

 This is what I looked like about 500 million years ago (I'd just got my first fish!).

The plates float on my magma. And because the magma moves, the plates move too. Sometimes they bump together; sometimes they pull apart. And when they do, they change shape a bit.

If you spread me out flat, this is what my plates look like now – but they're still moving.

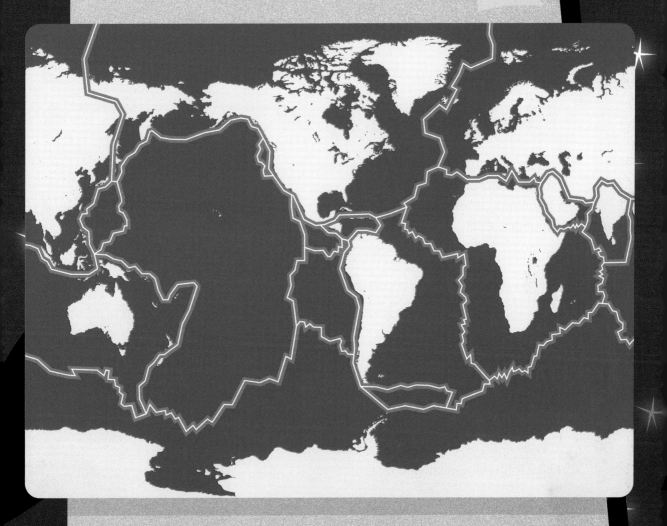

The movement of my plates is called 'plate tectonics'. The edges of my plates can be thick and have land on them – these are called **continental plates**. Or they can be thin and under oceans – these are called **oceanic plates**.

1 Continental >< Continental

When two continental plates crash together, they squash into each other, and my crust crumples and breaks. You get earthquakes – and mountains!

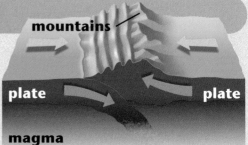

2 Oceanic <> Oceanic

When two of my oceanic plates move apart, magma comes to the surface in the space. Undersea mountains, including volcanoes, are formed.

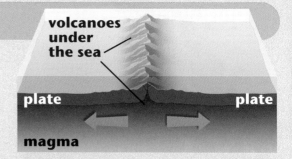

3 Oceanic >< Continental

When an oceanic plate and a continental plate crash together, the oceanic plate is denser and heavier so it gets forced down into my magma. There, it melts, and causes earthquakes and volcanoes near the edge of the continental plate. Where it tips down, a deep ocean trench is made.

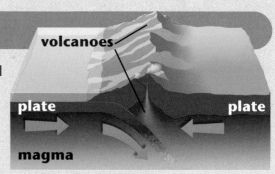

 Luckily, plates are created and melted at about the same rate, so I stay the same size!

This kind of activity produces volcanoes and earthquakes – in fact almost all volcanoes and earthquakes happen where my plates meet.

Plate tectonics quiz

My plates are still on the move. What kind of plate tectonics —
continental >< continental; oceanic <> oceanic; oceanic >< continental;
continental <> continental — is happening in each of these examples? Answers
on page 33 (no peeking!).

A India hit Asia about 50 million years ago. It is still moving north at a rate of 12 cm a year, squashing further into Asia — the Himalayas get about 2 cm higher every year!

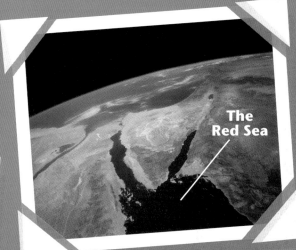

The
Red Sea

B The Arabian and African plates are moving. The Red Sea is widening by about 1 cm every year.

C Mountains are forming in the middle of the Atlantic Ocean.

Atlantic
Ocean

D The Andes is a range of volcanic mountains lying along the west coast of South America. There are still lots of earthquakes in this area.

Back to my life story

 Let's skip forward in time – this picture of me was taken only 250 million years ago.

About this time, all the plates that had dry land on them drifted together and made one huge continent, Pangaea.

Scientists named this supercontinent Pangaea *(say pan-guy-ah)* because in ancient Greek 'pan' means 'all' and 'gaea' means 'Earth' (me!).

Animal life on Pangaea

Because lots of volcanoes erupted while making Pangaea, a lot of animals died out. This was the biggest extinction known in my history – 95% of the kinds of animals I had died out, including these little sea creatures – trilobites.

Trilobite fossils

Hissing cockroach

Some animals survived. Sharks have been around for 390 million years, and this hissing cockroach, which is alive today, looks exactly like ones I had about 300 million years ago. But after this mass extinction, new animals evolved to suit the new habitats. Evolution explains the way animals change and become new kinds of animals over a long time. Lots of different animals can evolve from the same common ancestors.

evolution (say *ee-vol-oo-shun*) *noun:*
1 gradual change into something different.
2 the development of animals and plants from earlier or simple forms of life.

Half-reptile from 220 million years ago

Is this an ancestor of yours? It might be. This is a half-reptile – a creature that's evolved from reptiles but has some things about it which are more like mammals.

I got dinosaurs!

Then, about 200 million years ago, after the first mammals evolved, Pangaea started to break up. First it broke into two supercontinents, Gondwana and Laurasia, which moved apart from each other. This break up had a big effect on the evolution of animals and where you find them today.

**Pangaea
250 million years ago**

200 million years ago

An evolutionary
case history – marsupials

On Gondwana, marsupial mammals evolved over millions of years and spread across the supercontinent. Marsupials are a kind of mammal, but unlike most mammals they give birth to very tiny young. The young then live in pouches on their mums' tummies while they grow larger.

Then 160 million years ago, this huge continent began breaking up too. As Gondwana spilt up, its parts moved to areas with different kinds of climate.

*Koala bear –
a marsupial*

160 million years ago

Marsupials died out in **Africa** as their forest habitats became warmer, grassy savannahs.

45 million years ago, Antarctica separated from Australia and drifted to the South Pole. Being so cold there, all mammals died out, but you can find fossils of the marsupials that used to live there.

Today

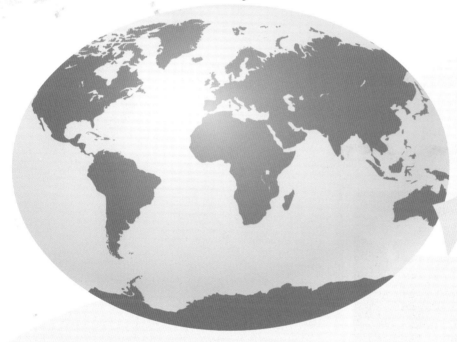

About 140 kinds of marsupial, including the kangaroo, live in Australia today.

Most South American marsupials died out when North American joined South America. North American mammals were stronger, faster and more intelligent than the marsupials who lived in the same habitats. For example, jaguars took over from the marsupial sabre-toothed tiger. There are only 72 kinds of marsupial left in South America today, and they are all small, night animals.

North America had been part of Laurasia, and didn't have any marsupials when it banged into South America 5 million years ago. When this happened, animals could cross between the two continents. Only one marsupial - the opossum - successfully moved into North America.

An evolutionary case history – islands

Island animals are often similar, but not identical, to animals living on the nearest mainland. This is because they have been cut off by the sea, and have evolved in slightly different ways from the animals on the mainland.

Islands that have been isolated for a very long time can evolve lots of very different new animals.

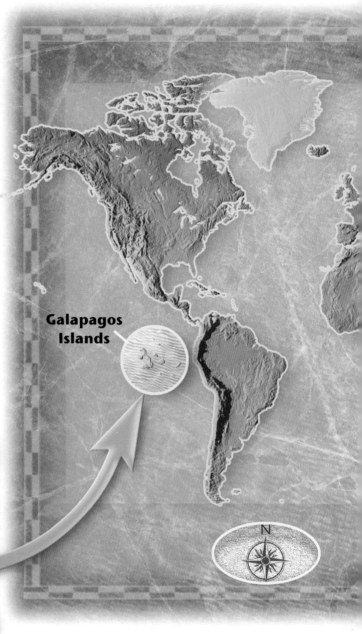

Galapagos Islands

Galapagos marine iguana

Galapagos marine iguanas are the only ones in the world that have adapted to swimming and getting food from the sea.

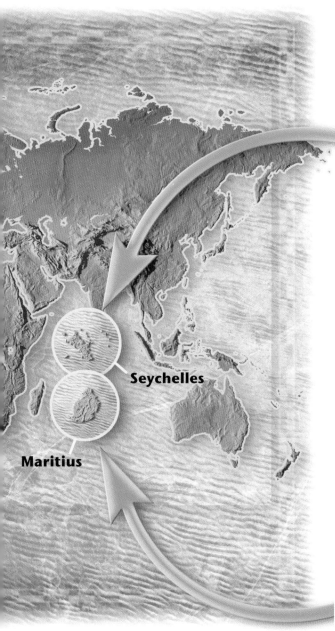

The coco de mer is the largest type of coconut in the world.

The Seychelles is a group of islands that broke away from India 65 million years ago. Since then, many different types of plants and animals have evolved that you can only find here.

Seychelles

Maritius

Dodos were flightless birds. They lived on Mauritius quite happily until people came, cut down their forest habitat, shot them for food, and brought cats, rats and pigs which ate their eggs. Dodos became extinct in the 17th century.

Dodo

So, to return to where we began: why are the animals of Bali and Lombok (islands only 25 km apart, remember) so different?

Because they are on two different plates, of course. Between these two islands lies the boundary between the Asian and Australian plates. There is a very deep trench between the plates, so that even with sea level changes there has never been a land bridge to allow animals to cross from one side to the other. In fact, some fish and even many kinds of birds refuse to cross the line.

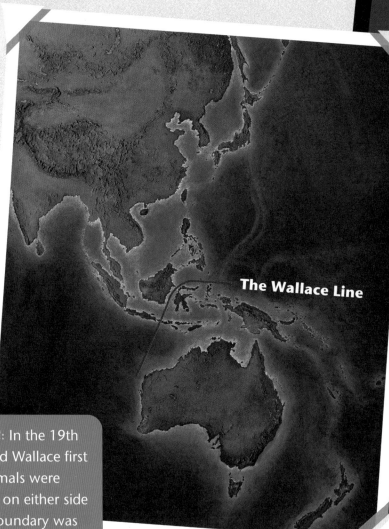

The Wallace Line

THE WALLACE LINE: In the 19th century, a man called Wallace first realised that the animals were completely different on either side of this line, so the boundary was named after him.

 This is what I may look like 200 million years in the future. Can you see what might have moved?

N

Glossary

continent   one of Earth's main masses of land

core   the innermost layer of the Earth

crust   the thin, outer surface of the Earth

evolution   the gradual changing of plants and animals from earlier or simpler forms through time

extinct   not existing any more

fossil   remains or traces of an ancient animal or plant that has been buried in the ground for a very long time and been hardened in rock

magma   hot molten rock in the mantle

mammal   an animal that is born alive and drinks milk from its mother

mantle   the layer of the Earth on which the crust floats

marsupial   a group of mammals which are born very early and are carried in pouches on their mother's stomachs when young

tectonic plates   sections of the Earth's crust that move independently

volcano   a mountain formed when tectonic forces cause the mantle to explode outwards.

Answers to quiz on pages 25
A Continental >< Continental;   **B** Continental <> Continental;
C Oceanic <> Oceanic;   **D** Oceanic >< Continental

Unit 3

THE CENTURY OF THE CAR

by Steve New

Introduction

What would your life be like without cars?
Cars, as we might recognise them, were invented in the 19th century, but it was the 20th century that was really the century of the car. The history of the 20th century shaped the development of the car – and the development of the car shaped the history of the 20th century.

In the 20th century:

- there were two world wars and military vehicles were first developed;
- man first walked and drove on the moon;
- the speed cars move at increased to hundreds of miles an hour;
- the computer was invented.

How cars have developed

First land speed record set at 39.24 mph
see Speed, page 40

First World War
see War, page 36

Second World War
see War, page 36

First fully functioning electron mechanical computer
see Mass production and computers, page 42

Opel-Patent-Motorwagen System Lutzmann

Model T Ford

Chevrolet

1898   **1901**   **1914 – 1918**   **1920**   **1939 – 1944**   **1940**   **1940s**

Cars in the year 2000 looked very different from the cars made at the start of the 20th century.
This is because:

- ways of making cars have changed;
- we can make cars which go fast and look good;
- people want different kinds of cars;
- people want to do different things in their cars.

The number of motor vehicles in the world could increase from 580 million in 1990 to 816 million in 2010. The USA owns about 40% of all the motor vehicles in the world. Car ownership is lowest in developing countries.

VW GOLF

The word 'car' comes from an ancient Celtic word 'carrus', meaning wagon or cart.

Chitty Chitty Bang Bang written – adventures of a flying car that can go on water
see Special cars, page 44

Moon buggy
see Special cars, page 44

Toyota Yaris

Buick

First air bags
see Safety, page 38

Michael Schumacher's first Grand Prix victory
see Speed, page 40

| 1960 | 1964 | 1971 | 1974 | 1980 | 1994 | 2000 |

War

The 20th century was a time of almost constant warfare around the world. *Special cars were needed for army use in wartime. They had to be strong and carry weapons. They also needed to be able to drive across fields and on roads that had been damaged by war.*

First World War 1914–1918

Cars were used on the battlefield for the first time in the First World War. *At the start of the war, normal domestic cars were used, with few changes other than the addition of a machine gun. As the war went on, the cars changed, with armour being added to the bodywork and chassis.*

Tanks

Tanks were first used in 1916. *Their tracks meant that they could drive off-road and across almost any terrain.*

Second World War 1939–1945

In 1942, domestic car production was interrupted, as many car manufacturers changed to making aircraft and military vehicles. *General Motors, a car company in the USA, made artillery shells, bombs, fuses, navigation equipment, machine guns and anti-aircraft guns in its car factories, as well as engines and vehicles for use in the war.*

Tanks and aircraft were also produced in car factories.

Armoured cars

The army needed armoured cars that were stronger than the cars used in the First World War. *Armoured cars had a turret and a gun and were usually based around the designs of existing cars and trucks. They were used as scouting vehicles – to gather information – rather than in battle, for which tanks were more suitable.*

Jeeps

In 1940, the US government asked car makers to design a fast, lightweight all-terrain vehicle that could be used in war. *The first successful model was nicknamed a 'jeep'. Jeep comes from 'GP' – General Purpose vehicle (although soldiers say JEEP stands for 'Just Enough Essential Parts'!).*

Jeep commissioned by US government in 1940 for production in 1941

Modern-day four-wheel drive car

The purpose of the jeep was to provide a rugged and reliable military vehicle that was cheap to make, and quick and easy to build. *In many jeeps, the engine provided power to all four wheels (instead of just two, as for most normal cars). This is one feature that helped jeeps to drive over rough terrain (and is why jeeps are called 'four-wheel drives').*

Look at the cars on the roads around you. How much have military cars influenced the design of cars today?

More Americans have died in car accidents than have been killed in all the wars the USA has ever fought.

Safety

As cars become more powerful, they can travel much faster. *The problem is that the faster cars are going, the more likely they are to be involved in accidents, and the more likely it is that people in cars will be hurt, or even killed. For this reason, safety features in cars are essential to our survival on the road.*

How many people do you think were killed or injured in your region last year? Try to find out.

The engine

There are normally four cylinders in a car engine. *Each of the cylinders goes through this four-stage cycle:*

1. Suck
The piston goes downwards, sucking fuel and air into the cylinder.

2. Squeeze
The piston goes upwards, squeezing the air and fuel ...

3. Bang!
... and then the spark plug sets fire to the fuel. The explosion forces the piston down, giving power to drive the car. For a car to work, there are thousands of explosions like this every minute.

4. Blow
The piston goes upwards again, blowing out the exhaust gas so the cycle can start again.

in valve

fuel & air sucked in here

Piston

SparkPLUG

BANG

the out valve

Air bags

The first air bags were fitted in 1974, but they only began to be widely used in the 1990s.

Seat belts

From 1967, all new cars in the UK had to be fitted with seat belts; *in 1983 it became compulsory to wear front seat belts, and from 1991 it was compulsory to wear them in back seats also.*

As roads get busier and cars get faster, these extra safety features have become more and more important.

In spite of all these improvements, the numbers of people killed and injured in road traffic accidents continues to grow.

Fuel

The fuel that drives most cars is petrol (also called gasoline). *It is made from crude oil, which comes from the ground. This oil is made from the remains of prehistoric trees that were crushed thousands of years ago. There is only a limited amount of oil, and one day it will run out.*

The oil is pumped from the ground ...

... and turned into petrol at an oil refinery.

Then it is transported to petrol stations.

Scientists and engineers are working hard to invent new ways of powering cars. *One possibility is to use electricity, by using special rechargeable batteries called 'fuel cells'. Other options include making a substitute for oil from plants or solar power.*

1980 GM Sunracer: solar-powered car

Speed

The first person in Great Britain to be charged with speeding was Walter Arnold of East Peckham, Kent. *Mr Arnold was travelling in town at* four times *the legal speed limit. But the limit in towns at this time (1896) was just 2 mph (miles per hour), so he was only doing 8 mph! He was caught by a policeman who gave chase – on a bicycle! He was fined one shilling (five pence) plus costs.*

International speed limits today

Different countries have different speed limits.				
Country	Motorways	Urban stretches	Dual carriageways	Built-up areas
USA & Canada	75 mph	70 mph	65 mph	25–35 mph
Australia	60–68 mph	60 mph	60 mph	30–35 mph
UK	70 mph	60 mph	70 mph	30 mph
Germany	81 mph	62 mph	81 mph	30 mph
France	80 mph	68 mph	69 mph	31 mph

*But cars can go a **LOT** faster than this.*

Formula One racing cars can travel at up to 200 mph but, because racetracks have curves and tight bends, average speeds are lower – around 120 mph. *To achieve these speeds on winding roads, the cars have wide tyres to grip the road surface.*

Michael Schumacher is a German Formula One driver. *He has competed in about 200 Grand Prix races and won over 70 of these – an astounding record. Most of his driving career has been with Ferrari.*

BREAKING SPEED RECORDS

This graph shows the land speed records from 1898 to 1997. *To achieve a land speed record, a car should be driven for one mile, turn around, refuel, then return the mile – all within one hour. The final speed is the average of the two runs.*

The increase in speed on the graph follows a fairly straight line and, from this, you could work out what the speed record might be in 2020.

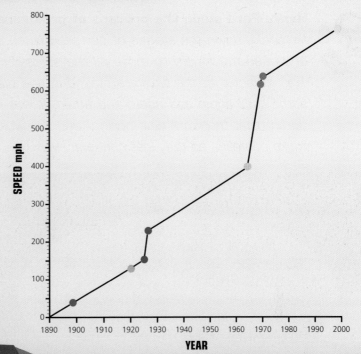

Speed of sound: 761 mph

After Thrust SSC (Super Sonic Car) broke the land speed record, the Queen sent a fax to the team. She wrote:

I am sure that I join Britons everywhere in congratulating you all on your tremendous achievement in setting a new land speed record. Your success, the culmination of six years of effort, is a source of great pride for the nation.

THE DRIVERS AND THEIR CARS

- M Chasseloup-Laubat, *Jeantauld Electric Car*
- Mr Kenelm Lee Guiness, *Sunbeam*
- Malcolm Campbell, *Sunbeam*
- Major Henry Seagrave, *Golden Arrow*
- Donald Campbell, *Bluebird*
- Gary Gabelich, *Blue Flame*
- Richard Noble, *Thrust II*
- Andy Green, *Thrust SSC*

Thrust SSC breaking the world land speed record in 1997, in Black Rock Desert

Mass production and computers

Henry Ford made the process of producing cars cheaper.
He broke down the stages of car production into small steps, and used machinery to move all the parts through the factory. This meant that the workers stayed in one place and did the same task again and again and again. It was very efficient, but meant that the work was boring, and the workers could easily make mistakes as they lost concentration.

The word car comes from an ancient celtic word 'carrus', meaning wagon or cart

Working at the factory is the same hard work every day, all the time, doing the same thing over and over. The noise and boredom are terrible – but the pay is better than anywhere else, and one day I might be able to buy one of these cars for myself.

Car prices
1900 Oldsmobile $650
1924 Model T Ford $290

Workers' wages at Ford
1913 $5 per day
1918 $6 per day

Since the first computer was built in 1946, technology has improved, so that more and more powerful and complicated computers have been made. *The things computers have been able to do has influenced what they have been used for.*

First electronic computer built (the size of a small room)

Floppy disk invented

Laptop computers produced

Microchip invented

First personal computers (PCs) on sale

Internet use widespread

| 1939 | 1959 | 1970 | 1975 | 1986 | 1990 |

Designers use computers to design cars. They use programs to do the mathematics to test that new models will work and will be safe.

When computers became widespread in the 1960s and 1970s, car makers began to use them to control the machines in the mass production factories. *By the end of the 20th century, many of the jobs that used to be done by people were done by computer-controlled robots instead. Robots are brilliant at doing the same job in exactly the same way each time, and are especially useful for welding metal parts together and painting cars.*

If computers and robots are used to make cars today, what happened to the people who used to do these jobs?

Computers are used to organise the factory and to make sure all the parts are available.

Computers are often used inside cars to help the driver plan journeys.

Computers control the robots that paint the car.

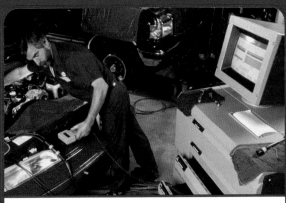

Mechanics use computers to measure how a car's engine is running.

About 20% of the cost of a car is the electronics.

Special cars
Moon buggy

Neil Armstrong was the first man to walk on the moon, on 21st July 1969. *He and his fellow Apollo astronauts were very limited as to how far they could explore. Walking on the moon is tiring and confusing; astronauts use a lot of oxygen and risk getting lost. In January 1971, astronauts of Apollo 14 left their lunar module to collect rocks from a 1 km-wide Cone Crater. Disorientated by the unfamiliar landscape, they couldn't find the crater, and gave up their search. They later discovered that they had been just 30 m from the rim of the crater. To help lunar exploration, it had already been decided that a moon buggy (a 'lunar roving module') should be taken up into space. In 1969 NASA asked people for ideas about what to build.*

It wasn't going to be easy.

NASA: National Aeronautics and Space Administration (USA)

Moon buggies must:
- work without air; without air a normal car engine cannot work (see Car power, page 39);
- work in temperatures that change from very hot to very cold;
- be small enough to fit in the lunar module;
- be easy to put together on the moon;
- be able to drive over the surface of the moon.

The successful design was taken up to the moon in Apollo 15 in July 1971. *It weighed 209 kg on Earth and 32 kg on the moon. Each wheel had its own motor. The battery-powered Lunar Rover could travel at 10–12 kph (about 7 mph).*

Lunar Roving Vehicle (LRV), used on Apollo 15, 16 and 17 missions

Cars that go on water

Cars that go on water as well as on land are not a new invention. *The first one was made in 1789, and the idea has been used for years in books and films. But now cars that go on water are actually for sale.*

Amphibious cars

In 1789, Oliver Evans designed his Oruckter Amphibolus – *a steam-powered, 21-ton wooden vehicle that could travel on both the streets and the waterways of Philadelphia, USA.*

Over 200 years later, in 2003, the Aquada was launched in Great Britain. *Looking like a sports car, it can go at up to 100 mph on land. With the press of a button the car is made suitable for water, where it can reach speeds of 35 mph. The Aquada has no roof (so it's not quite so waterproof in the rain!) and no doors – you have to jump in over the side.*

Cars like this have been the stuff of fiction for years. *In 1964, Ian Fleming wrote a series of stories for children about a magical car called Chitty Chitty Bang Bang – a twelve-cylinder, eight-litre, supercharged magical car which can fly and turn itself into a hovercraft.*

It is no coincidence that Fleming's other famous novels, the James Bond books, feature cars with amazing gadgets. *In the Bond film The Spy Who Loved Me, Bond's Lotus Esprit car turns into a submarine at the flick of a switch.*

1789 Oruckter Amphibolus – the first amphibious vehicle on record

2003 Aquada

As fiction becomes reality, how long will it be before we see family cars that can go on water?

Fictional cars

Cars play an important part in modern fiction, with car chases a regular feature of films. *The cars themselves might be nothing more than very fast regular cars, or they may have extra features added to make them more suitable for the hero's lifestyle – bullet-proof glass, ejector seats, computerised navigation systems, etc.*

How much do the gadgets in fictional cars inspire the designers of cars of the future? These are some of the cars from 'cult' fiction from 1960 to 2000.

Thunderbirds
Model *Rolls Royce*
1963

Notes: This pink car is usually driven by Parker, Lady Penelope's chauffeur. The car has six wheels, a see-through roof, rocket launchers and a machine gun.

James Bond in Tomorrow Never Dies
Model *BMW 750i*
1997

Notes: Bond's cars always come fitted with amazing gadgets. This one has remote control, armour, missiles, an on-board computer and a device that sheds tyre-shredding tacks to stop other cars giving chase.

Knight Rider
Model *Pontiac Trans-Am*
1982

Notes: This car (called 'KITT') has top speeds of 300 mph. It has a computer with a voice, a turbojet, auto-cruise, auto-pursuit, auto-collision avoidance and an emergency eject button.

The future of the car

Design and features

? *What new gadgets will cars have by the end of the 21st century?*

Cars with computerised navigation systems are now more common. *Electronics have taken the effort out of locking cars, opening windows and opening sunroofs. New devices are being fitted to help drivers park their cars in towns – including one new car that shrinks down from being a four-seater to a two-seater so it's easier to park.*

Safety

? *Will cars get safer?*

The technology to make cars go faster is available, but can we go faster on motorways and still be safe? *Many accidents are caused by a lack of concentration, so 'cruise systems' are being developed. These allow the road and the car to 'talk' to each other, giving information about dangerous objects or situations, stopping the driver from accidentally driving out of the lane and generally avoiding crashes.*

Fuel

? *What will power cars in the year 2100?*

With concerns that fossil fuels will run out in the next 50 years, new fuels are being researched. *If a plant-oil substitute fuel is found, the countryside might change as fields of the plant fuel stretch across the countryside. Will future car fuels change our whole landscape?*

Rinspeed Presto (shrinking car for parking), before ...

... and after!

Speed

? *Will cars get faster?*

Cars are capable of greater and greater speeds. *But as roads have got busier, average speeds in towns have slowed down again – in London, the average speed at the end of the 20th century was no greater than the speed at the beginning of the century, when most people were not using cars.*

What will **you** be driving?

The Car Trip

Mum says:
'Right, you two,
this is a very long car journey.
I want you two to be good.
I'm driving and I can't drive properly
if you two are going mad in the back.
Do you understand?'

So we say,
'OK, Mum, OK. Don't worry'
and off we go.

And we start The Moaning:
Can I have a drink?
I want some crisps.
Can I open my window?
He's got my book.
Get off me.
Ow, that's my ear!

And Mum tries to be exciting:
 'Look out the window
There's a lamp-post.'

And we go on with The Moaning:
Can I have a sweet?
He's sitting on me.
Are we nearly there?

Don't scratch.
You never tell him off.
Now he's biting his nails.
I want a drink. I want a drink.

GR

And Mum tries to be exciting again:
'Look out the window
there's a tree.'

And we go on:
My hands are sticky.
He's playing with the doorhandle
now.
I feel sick.
Your nose is all runny.
Don't pull my hair.
He's punching me, Mum,
that's really dangerous, you know.
Mum, he's spitting.

And Mum says:
'Right I'm stopping the car.
I AM STOPPING THE CAR.'

She stops the car.

'Now, if you two don't stop it
I'm going to put you out the car
and leave you by the side of the road.'

He started it.
I didn't. He started it.

'I don't care who started it
I can't drive properly
if you two go mad in the back.
Do you understand?'

And we say:
'OK, Mum, OK, don't worry.'

Can I have a drink?

Michael Rosen

Here Comes the Sun

Introduction

The Sun is just one of the 100 billion stars that make up our galaxy, the Milky Way. There are many stars that are hundreds of times bigger and millions of times more powerful, but to us, the Sun is the most important star. Without it, life on Earth would not exist.

People have always made up stories about where the sun came from. Here are three sun stories from different parts of the world.

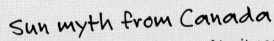

Sun myth from Canada

This tale comes from a tribe of Inuit people who live in the Arctic Circle, in the far north of Canada. For half the year they live in twilight because the sun never comes above the horizon. For the other half of the year there is always light. This tale gives one explanation of how this might have come about.

In myths, the relationship between animals and humans is often a central theme. This contrasts with *fables*, where animals are used instead of humans to tell a story which usually ends with a moral; for example, Aesop's fable *The Hare and the Tortoise*.

Animals in myths may be able to speak, they may have magical powers and they may be wise. They often help humans. Sometimes help is offered in return for something the human can do for the animal; sometimes it is given freely, and sometimes the help benefits both humans and the animal. This Canadian story is about a crow. Crows are killed in many countries. People think they are disgusting birds because they eat dead meat. The tale gives an explanation of why the Inuit do not kill crows.

NORTH POLE

ARCTIC CIRCLE
CANADA

Myths are ancient traditional stories of gods or heroes which address a concern of many people. They often try to explain events that occur in nature.

The Sun is just a middle-sized star, but to us it's life.

The Crow Brings the Daylight

At the beginning of time, the people lived in darkness. All year round. They could not see the distant hills, the animals to hunt, nor the stalking polar bear until it was upon them.

There lived then a wise old crow, who told the people stories of his youth, when he flew on journeys far and wide. Their favourite was his story about a land where you could see for miles and miles because of a special light – 'daylight' he called it.

If we had daylight, we could see to hunt, they said. We could see the polar bear from far away and defend ourselves or run. Please, Old Crow, they said, please go and find the land of daylight again and bring us back some light.

But the crow would not go. He was too tired and too old, he said. Old enough to stay at home for the rest of his days.

But the people kept begging him and pleading with him until at last he said he would go, if only to shut them up.

He flew far, far away until he saw daylight creeping through the darkness. He flew on until the world was bathed in its light. He looked down on a snowy landscape and saw that the light seemed to come from the snowhouse of a chief.

The chief's daughter was collecting water from the stream that ran beside the snowhouse. The crow turned itself into a speck of dust and settled itself gently onto the sealskin cape that she was wearing. Together they went into the snowhouse.

The dust-crow looked around. The chief was there, playing with his baby grandson by the fire. By his loving gestures and proud talk the crow knew that the chief was very fond of his grandson, and with that knowledge he hatched a plan.

The speck of dust floated off the daughter's cape and drifted across the snowhouse into the baby's ear. There it scratched and itched until the baby cried.

'Tell your grandfather that you want to play with the daylight,' whispered the crow in the baby's ear.

The baby did so. Now, the chief knew that the daylight was his prize possession, but he could not say no to his grandson. So he went to a carved wooden box and opened it. He took out a ball of daylight and tied it on the end of a string so that the baby could dangle the ball.

The baby gurgled with glee as he played with the ball. But the speck of dust began to scratch and itch again until the baby cried.

'Tell your grandfather that you want to play outside,' whispered the crow in the baby's ear.

The baby did so. Now, the chief could not say no to his grandson. He picked up the baby and carried him out into the snowy land, and the daylight ball swayed gently on its string.

The Inuit live in such cold conditions that they depend on warm clothing for survival.

- Caribou fur is used by the Inuit on their clothes to keep warm.
- Traditional Inuit jackets are called parkas.
- The Inuit wear insulated boots to keep their feet warm in freezing weather.

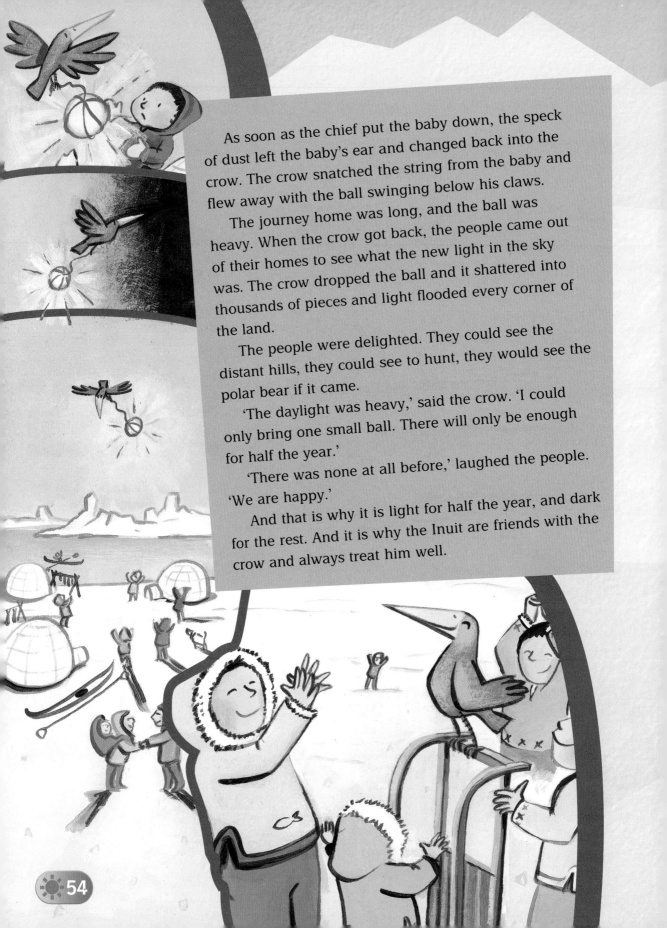

As soon as the chief put the baby down, the speck of dust left the baby's ear and changed back into the crow. The crow snatched the string from the baby and flew away with the ball swinging below his claws.

The journey home was long, and the ball was heavy. When the crow got back, the people came out of their homes to see what the new light in the sky was. The crow dropped the ball and it shattered into thousands of pieces and light flooded every corner of the land.

The people were delighted. They could see the distant hills, they could see to hunt, they would see the polar bear if it came.

'The daylight was heavy,' said the crow. 'I could only bring one small ball. There will only be enough for half the year.'

'There was none at all before,' laughed the people. 'We are happy.'

And that is why it is light for half the year, and dark for the rest. And it is why the Inuit are friends with the crow and always treat him well.

Sun myth from Australia

This is a sun creation story from south-east Australia. It is told by an Aborigine tribe who have lived in Australia for 50,000 years.

There are many different Aboriginal myths about the creation of the oceans and of humans, but not of the Earth itself. This may be because the Aborigine peoples call the earliest time in the world Dreamtime, which went on forever before the arrival of people.

This story offers explanations of some natural events – of why an Australian bird, the kookaburra, tends to sing just before dawn, and why there is a bright star in the sky before dawn.

The name kookaburra comes from one of the many Aboriginal names for the bird, and sounds like the harsh call it makes. In this story the kookaburra is called Gourgourgahgah – another way of writing down the call it makes.

The planet Venus is the brightest object in the sky after the sun and the moon. It has been called the morning star and the evening star in many different cultures because its bright light can be seen low in the sky at dawn and at dusk.

Kookaburras are known as the laughing jackasses of Australia. They live in dry forest and savannah (grassland) and eat insects and small animals such as snakes and lizards, which they kill by dropping them from a great height. Kookaburras 'laugh' as they go to roost at dusk and when they wake at dawn. They wake everyone else up too, so they are known as the 'bushman's clock'.

The Kookaburra and the Sun

When Earth was in Dreamtime, before people came into the world, the animals lived in darkness. Snakes slithered in the gloom of the stars and kangaroos hopped in the constant night of the pale moonlight across the eerie desert.

Gourgourgahgah the kookaburra sat in the branch of a tree. He called his loud cry.

'Kooo-Kaaa-Buuuu-Raaaaaaaaa!' he called.

Dinewan, the emu, was woken up and jumped from her large nest on the desert's sandy floor.

'Shut up!' she shouted. 'You woke me up, you noisy, selfish bird.'

'It's time to wake up,' said Gourgourgahgah.

'How do you know?' asked Dinewan, staring up at the black sky. 'How can we tell?'

Bralgah, the crane, agreed with Gourgourgahgah.

'You're just lazy,' she said to Dinewan.

Kooo-Kaaa Buuuu-Raaaaa!

Well, that started an argument – one of many between the birds. This was a long and bitter one. Bralgah got so cross with the emu that she flew down and grabbed one of Dinewan's eggs from her nest.

'Give it back!' screamed Dinewan, but instead the crane flung the egg as high as she could into the sky.

The egg soared and soared, up and up, and landed with a crack on a huge pile of wood in the sky.

The egg broke, the glistening yellow yolk seeped out – and set fire to the wood!

All the animals stared up at the fire in the sky. It was beautiful! It was warm! And best of all, it lit up the desert all around them. They could see! The birds were so happy they forgot to argue.

A good spirit in the sky, a cloud man called Ngoudenout, saw the fire, and saw how happy it made the animals on the Earth below.

'How much nicer the world would be with light,' he thought, and he flew to the fire.

'I will dampen it every evening so that the animals can sleep,' he decided. 'During the night I'll gather more firewood. And then every morning I'll light the fire, so they can see.'

On the evening of that first day, Ngoudenout dampened the fire as he had said he would, and the animals lay down to sleep. Ngoudenout began gathering firewood for the next day. Suddenly, he stopped.

'What will the animals think when they are woken up by a huge fire? Will they be frightened?' Ngoudenout thought and thought and came up with an idea.

'I will make a Morning Star, a bright shining star that will remind all the creatures that the day is coming,' he said.

So Ngoudenout made the Morning Star and it shone brightly in the East. But as he was preparing to light the fire, the spirit looked down at the Earth. He saw that many of the animals were still sleeping and could not see the Morning Star. Ngoudenout thought again, and had an even brighter idea. He called to the kookaburra, who was already awake.

'Oh Gourgourgahgah, will you laugh your call in the morning, just before I light the fire? That way everyone will be awake when the fire lights up the sky, and so they won't be afraid of it.'

And the kookaburra still does so from that day to this.

The Aborigines also say that any child that insults a kookaburra will grow an extra slanting tooth.

Sun myth from Greece

Rather than the sun being made from an object, as in the previous stories, for the Ancient Greeks the sun was a god.

For thousands of years, the Greeks invented and reinvented myths about how the universe began. Some of them have got mixed up and muddled over time. The very early Greeks believed that the universe came out of an emptiness called Chaos.

Over time, Greece changed and new gods were invented to fit new ideas. The Greeks invented a group of gods called the Titans.

A male sun god, Helios, was the son of two Titan gods. He rode a chariot of four horses across the sky every day. At night, he slept in the cabin of a golden ship, as he was taken back to the East on the ocean that the Greeks thought at this time went all around the Earth.

Even later, a new generation of Greeks invented new generations of gods. The Greeks began to worship a group of gods who lived on Mount Olympus, and were ruled by Zeus.

Apollo is one of these Olympian gods. For a while, he was known in some parts of the Greek Empire as the god of light, and he existed side by side with Helios. But, over time, stories of Apollo and Helios got mixed up and they became one god.

Later still, the Romans worshipped this Apollo too.

As well as being the sun god, Apollo was the god of music, archery, healing, plague, prophecy and truth (and mice!). He was also the Greeks' idea of perfect masculine beauty.

This is the story of his birth.

GREECE

Apollo was one of the 12 Greek Olympian gods. One of his most important daily tasks was to harness his chariot with four horses and drive the sun across the sky.

The Twins: Sun and Moon

'You can't stay here,' said the voice, as yet another door was closed gently on her.

Leto turned away and walked down to the shore. For months now she had been travelling, trying to find a place where she could rest and have her babies. But no one would let her stay.

'They're frightened of what Hera might do to them,' she reminded herself again. 'Of course they can't let me stay.'

The queen of the gods, Hera, had heard that Leto was expecting twins. And she knew that it was her husband, Zeus, who had made Leto pregnant. In a fit of jealousy, Hera had decreed that no one should let Leto stay with them anywhere under the sun. And so Leto was turned away at every door.

Leto sat on the shore. She wept as she stared out to sea. What could she do next? Where could she go? Then, through her tears, Leto saw something strange coming across the waves. A small island seemed to be floating towards her! As she stood and wiped her tears away, Poseidon, the god of the sea, came to her.

'I've made an island for you, Leto,' he said. 'I'll shade it with my waves and you'll be safe from Hera.'

Poseidon was Zeus's brother, so maybe that is why he took pity on the beautiful goddess.

Leto stepped onto the floating island of Delos. One palm tree grew at its centre. Thanking Poseidon, Leto sank down to rest against its trunk.

Delos floated across the seas as Leto rested.

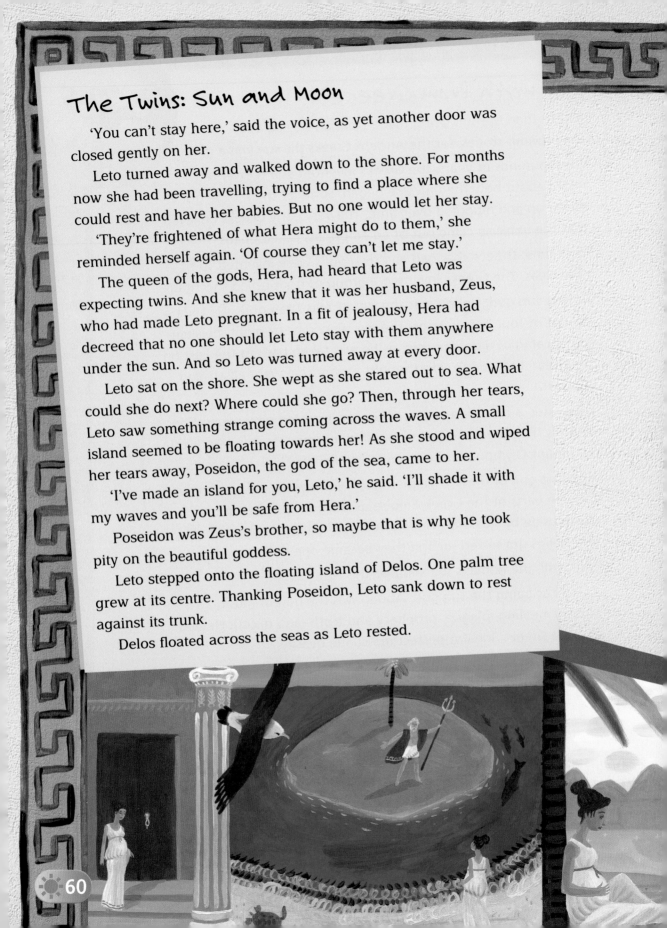

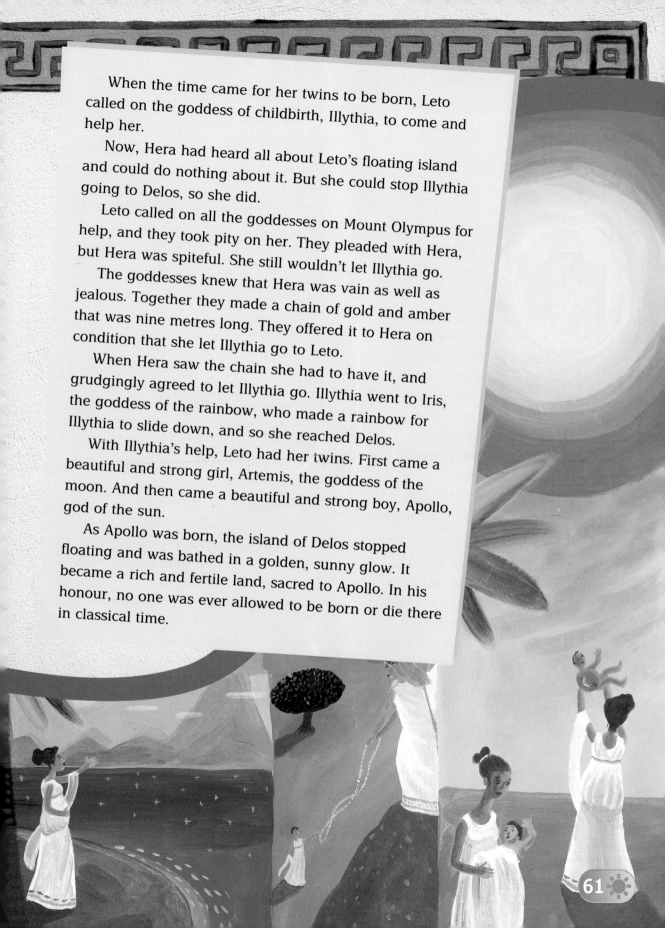

When the time came for her twins to be born, Leto called on the goddess of childbirth, Illythia, to come and help her.

Now, Hera had heard all about Leto's floating island and could do nothing about it. But she could stop Illythia going to Delos, so she did.

Leto called on all the goddesses on Mount Olympus for help, and they took pity on her. They pleaded with Hera, but Hera was spiteful. She still wouldn't let Illythia go.

The goddesses knew that Hera was vain as well as jealous. Together they made a chain of gold and amber that was nine metres long. They offered it to Hera on condition that she let Illythia go to Leto.

When Hera saw the chain she had to have it, and grudgingly agreed to let Illythia go. Illythia went to Iris, the goddess of the rainbow, who made a rainbow for Illythia to slide down, and so she reached Delos.

With Illythia's help, Leto had her twins. First came a beautiful and strong girl, Artemis, the goddess of the moon. And then came a beautiful and strong boy, Apollo, god of the sun.

As Apollo was born, the island of Delos stopped floating and was bathed in a golden, sunny glow. It became a rich and fertile land, sacred to Apollo. In his honour, no one was ever allowed to be born or die there in classical time.

Hiawatha's Childhood

By the shores of Gitche Gumee,
By the shining Big-Sea-Water,
Stood the wigwam of Nokomis,
Daughter of the Moon, Nokomis.
Dark behind it rose the forest,
Rose the black and gloomy pine-trees,
Rose the firs with cones upon them;
Bright before it beat the water,
Beat the clear and sunny water,
Beat the shining Big-Sea-Water.

There the wrinkled, old Nokomis
Nursed the little Hiawatha,
Rocked him in his linden cradle,
Bedded soft in moss and rushes,
Safely bound with reindeer sinews;
Stilled his fretful wail by saying,
'Hush! the Naked Bear will get thee!'
Lulled him into slumber, singing,
'Ewa-yea! my little owlet!
Who is this that lights the wigwam?
With his great eyes lights the wigwam?
Ewa-yea! my little owlet!'

Many things Nokomis taught him
Of the stars that shine in heaven;
Showed him Ishkoodah, the comet,
Ishkoodah, with fiery tresses;
Showed the Death-Dance of the spirits
Warriors with their plumes and war-clubs,

Flaring far away to northward
In the frosty nights of Winter;
Showed the broad, white road in heaven,
Pathway of the ghosts, the shadows,
Running straight across the heavens,
Crowded with the ghosts, the shadows.

At the door on summer evenings
Sat the little Hiawatha;
Heard the whispering of the pine-trees,
Heard the lapping of the water,
Sound of music, words of wonder;
'Minne-wawa!' said the pine trees,
'Mudway-aushka!' said the water.

Saw the firefly, Wah-wah-taysee,
Flitting through the dusk of evening,
With the twinkle of its candle
Lighting up the brakes and bushes;
And he sang the song of children,
Sang the song Nokomis taught him:
'Wah-wah-taysee, little firefly,
Little, flitting, white-fire insect,
Little dancing, white-fire creature,
Light me with your little candle,
Ere upon my bed I lay me,
Ere in sleep I close my eyelids!'

Saw the moon rise from the water
Rippling, rounding from the water,
Saw the flecks and shadows on it,
Whispered, 'What is that, Nokomis?'
And the good Nokomis answered:
'Once a warrior, very angry,
Seized his grandmother, and threw her
Up into the sky at midnight;
Right against the moon he threw her;
'Tis her body that you see there.'

Saw the rainbow in the heaven,
In the eastern sky the rainbow,
Whispered, 'What is that, Nokomis?'
And the good Nokomis answered:
'Tis the heaven of flowers you see there;
All the wild-flowers of the forest,
All the lilies of the prairie,
When on earth they fade and perish,
Blossom in that heaven above us.'

When he heard the owls at midnight,
Hooting, laughing in the forest,
'What is that?' he cried in terror;
'What is that?' he said, 'Nokomis?'
And the good Nokomis answered:
'That is but the owl and owlet,
Talking in their native language,
Talking, scolding at each other.'

Then the little Hiawatha
Learned of every bird its language,
Learned their names and all their secrets,
How they built their nests in Summer,
Where they hid themselves in Winter,
Talked with them whene'er he met them,
Called them 'Hiawatha's Chickens'.

Of all beasts he learned the language,
Learned their names and all their secrets,
How the beavers built their lodges,
Where the squirrels hid their acorns,
How the reindeer ran so swiftly,
Why the rabbit was so timid,
Talked with them whene'er he met them,
Called them 'Hiawatha's Brothers'.

Henry Wadsworth Longfellow

63

Travel Trivia

Introduction

Thinking of a holiday? This unit includes facts about six countries in the world. Have a look through the statistics, read the information and see which ones you would like to visit.

As you flip through the countries, think about these questions:

Which country:
- is the biggest?
- is the smallest?
- has borders with most other countries?
- has borders with no countries?
- has no natural resources?

MONACO
page 74

ALGERIA
page 66

GUATEMALA
page 68

N

W   E

S

In which country:
- can the lowest percentage of people read?
- is the tallest mountain?
- is the lowest place?

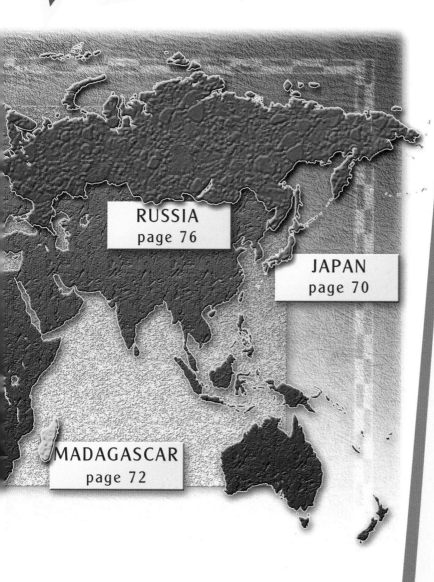

RUSSIA
page 76

JAPAN
page 70

MADAGASCAR
page 72

Notes about the tables in this unit

Capital the city where the Government works

Earnings the amount of money that the average person earns each year in that country. This figure is given in US dollars for all countries, so that you can compare them easily.

Languages the 'official' language is the language of government.

Life expectancy the average number of years you can expect to live if you were born in this country. Life expectancy helps people to measure the overall quality of life in a country.

Reading if a country has only a small percentage of people who can read, it can make it more difficult for the country to develop.

Natural resources things in or on the ground, or in water, that a country can use or sell, such as oil, timber and fish

ALGERIA

Algeria, the second largest country in Africa, has thousands of years of history to explore.

PEOPLE

NATIONALITY
Algerian

POPULATION
32,818,500

LANGUAGES
Arabic (official), French, Berber

% OF PEOPLE WHO CAN READ AT AGE 15
70

AVERAGE AMOUNT EARNED EACH YEAR PER PERSON (IN US$)
5300

LIFE EXPECTANCY (IN YEARS)
70.5

RELIGION
Muslim 99%
Christian and Jewish 1%

A Climb among the deep valleys and rocky cliffs here and you can find thousands of cave paintings, dating from 12,000 BC to 100 AD.

See buildings made the traditional way, from desert earth.

What the guidebooks don't tell you ...

If you drive into the desert, make sure your car is working properly, and always know where you are on a map – it's very easy to get lost. ALWAYS take plenty of water.

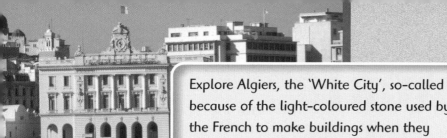

Explore Algiers, the 'White City', so-called because of the light-coloured stone used by the French to make buildings when they ran Algeria in the 19th and 20th centuries. Haggle for trinkets in the kasbah.

SPAIN

Mediterranean Sea

Algiers

MOROCCO

B

TUNISIA

ALGERIA

Sahara Desert

MAURITANIA

A LIBYA

N

MALI

NIGER

GEOGRAPHY

CONTINENT
Africa

CAPITAL
Algiers

AREA (IN KM²)
2,381,740

BORDERS WITH
Libya, Mali, Mauritania, Morocco, Niger, Tunisia, Western Sahara, Mediterranean Sea

LOWEST AND HIGHEST PLACES
LOWEST:
Chott Melrhir -40 m
HIGHEST:
Tahat 3003 m

CLIMATE
NORTH:
Max: 30 °C   Min: 16 °C
Rainfall per year: 700 mm
SOUTH:
Max: 36 °C   Min: 21 °C
Rainfall per year: 2 mm

NATURAL RESOURCES
Oil, gas, metals, minerals

NATURAL HAZARDS
Earthquakes and mudslides

B

In this area there are several well-preserved Roman cities. You will find forums, theatres, temples and arches – even the remains of houses. St Augustine of Hippo lived here 389–430. You can see the mosaics he walked upon, the Roman baths he used, and visit a cathedral named after him.

Take a camel caravan into the Sahara Desert and drink mint tea with the Tuareg tribespeople.

Guatemala

Two thousand years ago, Guatemala was part of the Mayan civilisation. The Mayans were a cultured people, who understood astronomy and mathematics, made amazing buildings (all without metal tools) and had a complicated writing system. But they never invented the wheel!

PEOPLE

Nationality
Guatemalan

Population
13,909,384

Languages
Spanish (official),
23 American
Indian languages

**% of people
who can read
at age 15**
70.6

**Average amount
earned each year
per person (in US$)**
3700

**Life expectancy
(in years)**
65.2

Religion
Christian,
American Indian beliefs

Go trekking or birdwatching among Guatemala's 37 volcanoes – but be careful, some are still active! You can tell the active ones by their bare peaks and the ash clouds rising from the craters … you can often see lava flowing down Pacaya, only 29 km from Guatemala City. One volcano even has a Mayan fortress in its crater!

Everything is colourful in Guatemala. The churches, the clothes – even the food!

Visit the ruined rainforest city of Tikal. About 100,000 Mayan people lived here 2000 years ago, ruled by the Jaguar clan lords. Climb the steps of temples and visit the baths and houses. As you journey through the jungle, see if you can spot any wildlife – howler monkeys, toucans, ocelots or even the jaguar.

GEOGRAPHY

Continent
North/Central America

Capital
Guatemala City

Area (in km²)
108,890

Borders with
Belize, El Salvador, Honduras, Mexico, Pacific Ocean, Caribbean Sea

Lowest and highest places
Lowest:
Pacific Ocean 0 m
Highest:
Volcan Tajumulco 4211 m

Climate
Max: 29 °C
Min: 12 °C
Rainfall per year:
1188 mm

Natural resources
Oils, metals, timber, fish

Natural hazards
Volcanoes, earthquakes, hurricanes

What the guidebooks don't tell you ...

There are 5000–10,000 street kids sleeping rough in Guatemala City. They have a very hard life, so it's no wonder that they pick pockets.

Japan

Japan can be the noisiest, or the most serene, place on the planet – if you know where to go.

People

Nationality
Japanese

Population
127,214,499

Language
Japanese

% of people who can read at age 15
99

Average amount earned each year per person (in US$)
28,000

Life expectancy (in years)
80.9

Religion
Shinto, Buddhist

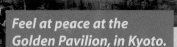
Feel at peace at the Golden Pavilion, in Kyoto.

Take a stroll in Tokyo – see the talking streetlights, talking adverts, video arcades galore, the latest hi-tech gadgets and fashion, thousands of cars and thousands more people. Tokyo can be overwhelming.

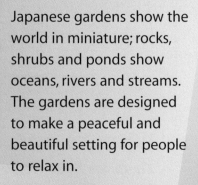

Japanese gardens show the world in miniature; rocks, shrubs and ponds show oceans, rivers and streams. The gardens are designed to make a peaceful and beautiful setting for people to relax in.

At the 17th-century Nijo Castle, there are floorboards that sound like a nightingale when you walk on them – they stopped assassins and eavesdroppers from getting too close!

CHINA
RUSSIA
NORTH KOREA
Pacific Ocean
SOUTH KOREA
Hiroshima
Kyoto
JAPAN
Tokyo
Mt Fuji
N

On 6th August 1945, a hydrogen bomb was dropped on Hiroshima. The bomb was the beginning of the end of the Second World War, but the single bomb killed 130,000 people. Visit the Children's Peace Monument there and see the thousands of folded paper cranes (a type of bird) left by visitors as a symbol of peace. Fold one to leave yourself.

Paper cranes left at the children's peace monument.

Geography

Continent
Asia

Capital
Tokyo

Area (in km²)
377,835

Borders with
Pacific Ocean

Lowest and highest places
Lowest:
Hachiro-gata −4 m
Highest:
Mount Fuji 3778 m

Climate
Max: 25 °C
Min: 4 °C
Rainfall per year:
1525 mm in Tokyo

Natural resources
Minerals, fish

Natural hazards
Earthquakes, volcanoes, typhoons

What the guidebooks don't tell you ...

More than 127 million people live in Japan, so it gets very crowded. During the rush hour in major Japanese cities, the underground trains get so crowded that subway staff often have to push people in before the doors can close!

Madagascar

Madagascar is the fourth largest island in the world. It broke away from Africa some 65 million years ago, and many kinds of animals and plants evolved here that are not seen anywhere else in the world (see unit 2). Animals such as lemurs and two-thirds of the world's chameleons, together with many kinds of plants and trees, can only be found in Madagascar. Look for them in the tropical rainforest, where you get over 3.5 m of rain a year!

PEOPLE

Nationality
Malagasy

Population
16,979,744

Languages
French (official),
Malagasy (official)

% of people who can read at age 15
68.9

Average amount earned each year per person (in US$)
760

Life expectancy (in years)
56.1

Religion
Local beliefs,
Christian, Muslim

Madagascar used to have many strange, large animals, such as elephant birds and giant lemurs. All are now extinct, except the Nile crocodile ...

Find the Nile crocodile in the 96 km of underground passages and caverns in Madagascar known as the Crocodile Caves. Where some caves have collapsed, you can find lakes and sunken forests.

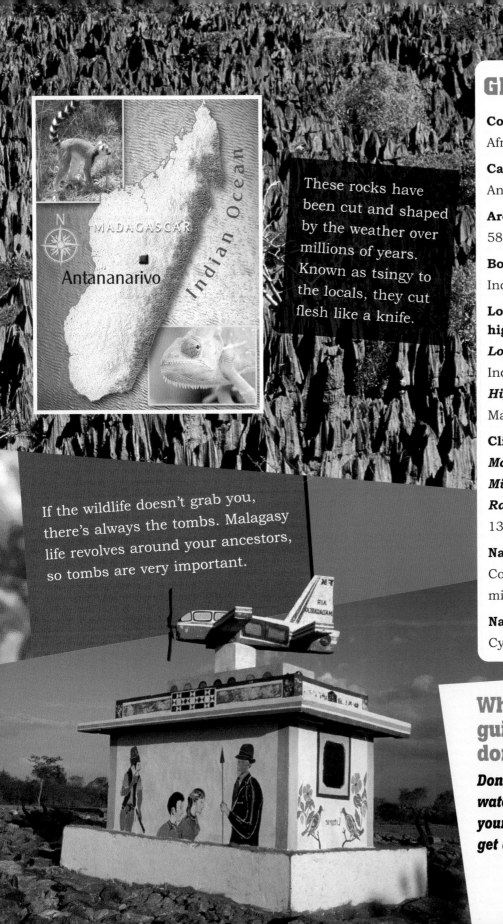

These rocks have been cut and shaped by the weather over millions of years. Known as tsingy to the locals, they cut flesh like a knife.

If the wildlife doesn't grab you, there's always the tombs. Malagasy life revolves around your ancestors, so tombs are very important.

GEOGRAPHY

Continent
Africa

Capital
Antananarivo

Area (in km²)
587,040

Borders with
Indian Ocean

Lowest and highest places
Lowest:
Indian Ocean 0 m
Highest:
Maromokotro 2876 m

Climate
Max: 21 °C
Min: 13 °C
Rainfall per year:
1370 mm

Natural resources
Coal, metals, minerals, fish

Natural hazards
Cyclones

What the guidebooks don't tell you ...

Don't drink the tap water, or have ice in your drinks. You may get a runny tummy!

Monaco

MONACO is called a 'principality', because it is an independent state with a Prince (Rainier III) at its head. Monaco is the second smallest independent state in the world, after the Vatican in Rome, where the Pope lives. The whole of the hilly country is one big city – Monte Carlo is a suburb of Monaco. There is no countryside at all!

FRANCE

ITALY

Monte Carlo casino

MONACO

Port of Monaco

Hotel de Paris

Mediterranean Sea

N

People

NATIONALITY	Monégasque
POPULATION	32,130
LANGUAGES	French (official), English, Italian, Monégasgne
% OF PEOPLE WHO CAN READ AT AGE 15	99
AVERAGE AMOUNT EARNED EACH YEAR PER PERSON (IN US$)	27,000
LIFE EXPECTANCY (IN YEARS)	79.3
RELIGION	Christian

Mingle with the rich and famous!

Geography

CONTINENT	Europe
CAPITAL	Monaco
AREA (IN KM^2)	1.95
BORDERS WITH	France, Mediterranean Sea
LOWEST AND HIGHEST PLACES	Lowest: Mediterranean Sea 0 m Highest: Mont Agel 140 m
CLIMATE	Max: 24 °C Min: 10 °C Rainfall per year 760 mm
NATURAL RESOURCES	None
NATURAL HAZARDS	None

Try your luck in the luxury casino – see if you can break the bank at Monte Carlo!

See and be seen at
THE ONLY PLACE TO BE ON THE RIVIERA!*

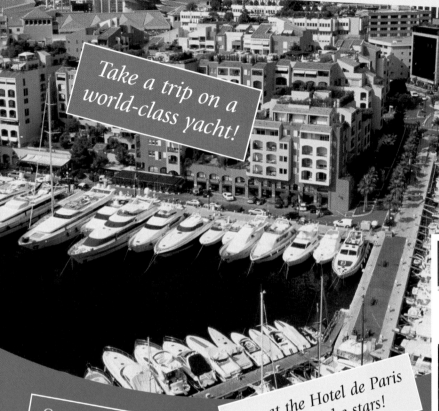

Take a trip on a world-class yacht!

Catch a glimpse of royalty!

Sun! Sea! Sand!

Stay at the Hotel de Paris – hotel of the stars!

*The Riviera is the name for the Mediterranean coast of France.

Watch as the world's fastest cars race through the streets of this delightful principality!

What the guidebooks don't tell you ...

 You don't get much for your euro here!

Russia

Russia is the largest country in the world. It includes part of Europe in the west, and Asia in the east. Because of the bitterly cold climate and harsh living conditions, there are relatively few people living here.

PEOPLE

Nationality
Russian

Population
144,526,278

Languages
Russian

% of people who can read at age 15
99.6

Average amount earned each year per person (in US$)
9300

Life expectancy (in years)
67.7

Religion
Christian, Muslim, Buddhist

St Petersburg is known as the 'Venice of the North' because of all its canals. The streets and canals of St Petersburg date back to when tsars (emperors) ruled the country. Here you can visit one of the most famous museums in the world – The Hermitage.

Stare at the preserved body of Lenin, once the leader of Russia. (Or is it a wax copy? You decide.)

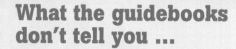

What the guidebooks don't tell you ...

One visitor says: 'I went to Moscow in the winter. It was so cold that every time I breathed in I could hear and feel my nose hairs cracking as they froze, and every time I breathed out I could feel the moisture as they unfroze again. And, in this weather, the Russians were eating ice creams in the street!'

Take the Trans-Siberian Express across Russia. Your six-day journey will take you 9446 km from Moscow to Vladivostok. You'll pass by endless forests, Lake Baikal – a lake as big as Belgium, the Siberian wastes and end up on the shores of the Pacific Ocean.

Journey from Vladivostock to the Kamchatka Peninsula, where you can see geysers, volcanoes and grizzly bears fishing for salmon.

If midnight sun is your thing, try Murmansk in the summer – or catch the Festival of the North, with reindeer racing and skiing in March.

GEOGRAPHY

Continent
Europe and Asia

Capital
Moscow

Area (in km²)
17,075,200

Borders with
Azerbaijan, Belarus, China, Estonia, Finland, Georgia, Kazakhstan, North Korea, Latvia, Lithuania, Mongolia, Norway, Poland, Ukraine

Lowest and highest places
Lowest:
Caspian Sea −28 m
Highest:
Mount Elbrus 5633 m

Climate
Max: 16 °C
Min: −10 °C

Rainfall per year
630 mm in Moscow

Natural resources
Oil, gas, coal, metals, minerals, timber

Natural hazards
Permafrost (ground that is always frozen) in Siberia, volcanoes in Kuril Islands, earthquakes, floods, forest fires

A Kingdom of Castles

There's a glossary of castle words on page 93.

Introduction

There are castles everywhere in the United Kingdom, built over hundreds of years to protect kings, queens and rich nobles.

Castles were built at strategic points – places which would have the advantage in a battle. Strategic points would be places:

◆ on high ground where you could see the enemy coming;
◆ on a road or river crossing;
◆ with natural defences, e.g. cliffs.

Motte and bailey castles

The earliest castles you can still see all around the UK are motte and bailey castles from the 11th century.

Why build a motte and bailey castle?

Advantages of a motte:

♦ you can see your enemy coming and fire down at them;
♦ it's quick and easy to build.

Advantages of a bailey:

♦ soldiers live in a large, protected area. In an attack, everyone squeezes into the keep;
♦ livestock is protected.

How to improve motte and bailey castles:

♦ build a stone tower, or 'keep', on the motte, and a wall around the bailey (wooden fences burn);
♦ build a parapet wall around your roof to protect the lookout;
♦ build crenellations. (In the 11th century, you needed a licence to crenellate your castle. The King only wanted his friends to have them.);
♦ make arrow slits;
♦ flood the ditch and make a moat;
♦ protect the entrance – the weakest part of any castle.

Cardiff Castle, South Glamorgan, Wales

The Romans built a fort at Cardiff. Most of the buildings in Cardiff Castle today are Victorian, and were built to make the castle look like a fairy tale castle.

The motte and bailey inside Cardiff Castle was built in 1091. The 12 m-high motte was built over a rocky hillock and was, at first, protected with wooden fencing. In the 12th century, the motte was topped with a 12-sided stone keep. The smaller gate tower at the front was built in the 15th century.

The Legend of King Arthur

In the middle of the 15th century, a knight called Thomas Malory collected together all the stories he had heard about the first Christian king, who was known as King Arthur. Stories of King Arthur were told in France and Wales as well as in England. King Arthur was a Christian who fought against the pagan Saxons. Malory wrote that King Arthur was 'the moost renomed Crysten kyng, ... whyche ought moost to be remembred emonge us Englysshemen tofore al other Crysten kynges'. Many of the stories of King Arthur and the Knights of the Round Table tell of their adventures as they attack and defend castles in Wales and the west of England.

This part of the tale begins when King Arthur's father, King Uther Pendragon, was betrayed and Merlin, the wizard, came from his own castle, to help find the King's son and heir.

Years of strife and misery went by, until the appointed time was at hand. Then Merlin, the good enchanter, came out from the deep mysterious valleys of north Wales. Merlin came to London and spoke with the Archbishop; and a great gathering of knights was called for Christmas Day – so great that all of them could not find a place in the abbey church, so that some were forced to gather in the churchyard.

In the middle of the service, there arose suddenly a murmur of wonder outside the abbey: for there was seen, though no man saw it come, a great square slab of marble stone in the churchyard, and on the stone an anvil of iron, and set point downwards a great shining sword of steel thrust deeply into the anvil... Round about the anvil they found letters of gold set in the great stone, and the letters read thus: WHOSO PULLETH OUT THIS SWORD FROM THIS STONE AND ANVIL IS THE TRUE-BORN KING OF ALL BRITAIN.

When they saw this, many and many a man tried to pull out the sword, but not one of them could stir it a hair's breadth.

'He is not here,' said the Archbishop. 'But doubt not that God will send us our king. Upon New Year's Day we will hold a great tournament, and see whether our king is amongst those who come to joust. Until then, I counsel that we appoint ten knights to guard the stone, and set a rich pavilion over it.'

All this was done, and upon New Year's Day a great host of knights met together.

But none as yet could draw forth the sword out of the stone. Then they went all a little way off, and pitched tents, and held a tournament or sham-fight, trying their strength and skill at jousting with long lances of wood, or fighting with broad-swords.

It happened that among those who came was the good knight Sir Ector, and his son Kay, who had been made a knight not many months before; and with them came Arthur, Sir Kay's young brother, a youth of scarcely 16 years of age. Riding to the jousts, Sir Kay found suddenly that he had left his sword in his lodgings, and he asked Arthur to ride back and fetch it for him.

'Certainly I will,' said Arthur, who was always ready to do anything for other people, and back he rode to the town. But Sir Kay's mother had locked the door, and gone out to see the tournament, so that Arthur could not get into the lodgings at all.

This troubled Arthur very much. 'My brother Kay must have a sword,' he thought, as he rode slowly back. 'It will be a matter for unkind jests if so young a knight comes to the jousts without a sword. But where can I find him one? ... I know! I saw one sticking in an anvil in the churchyard, I'll fetch that: it's doing no good there!'

So Arthur set spurs to his horse and came to the churchyard. Tying his horse to the stile, he ran to the stone – and found that all ten of the guardian knights had also gone to the tournament. Without stopping to read what was written on the stone, Arthur pulled out the sword at a touch, ran back to his horse, and in a few minutes had caught up with Sir Kay and handed it over to him.

by Roger Lancelyn Green

Dunluce Castle, County Antrim, Northern Ireland

Romantic, crumbling Dunluce Castle has a history entangled with local folklore.

The castle perches on a 34 m-high volcanic rock which is joined to the mainland by a bridge. A sea cave, 'Mermaid's Cave', burrows under the castle.

Dunluce: history and legend

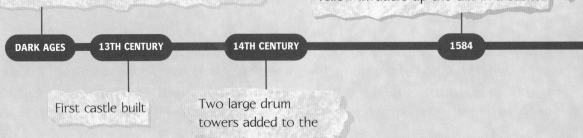

Early Irish ring-fort and underground chamber connecting to the sea cave below

Scottish chieftain, Sorley Boy MacDonnell, attacks and takes the castle. Legend has it that one of MacDonnell's men gets work in the castle and then hauls his fellow invaders up the cliff in a basket.

| DARK AGES | 13TH CENTURY | 14TH CENTURY | 1584 |

First castle built

Two large drum towers added to the

The Giant's Causeway

The Giant's Causeway is an area of alien-looking landscape just along the coast from Dunluce Castle. There are over 40,000 stone columns packed together like a huge honeycomb. The columns are mostly hexagonal, but some have four, five, seven or even eight sides. The tallest are 12 m high, and they look like steps down into the sea.

The Causeway was formed 50–60 million years ago, during a period of volcanic activity. Lava poured out of the ground and created these geometric columns as it cooled.

The *Girona*, a galleon of the Spanish Armada, is ship-wrecked in a storm on the Giant's Causeway, just along the coast from Dunluce, as it flees for home. Sorley Boy MacDonnell salvages the wreck and uses the money to improve the castle. He makes holes in the castle walls to fit in four of the *Girona's* cannons.

Siege! The Irish army destroys Dunluce village while laying siege (unsuccessfully) to the castle.

The castle is given to the nation for preservation.

1588   **1639**   **1641**   **LATE 17TH CENTURY**   **EARLY 20TH CENTURY**

Part of the castle, including the kitchens, falls into the sea. Legends say that all the pots and pans and seven cooks are swept away by the waves, but a poor cobbler is found safe, sleeping in the only surviving corner of the room.

The castle is abandoned.

The Legend of Finn MacCool and the Giant's Causeway

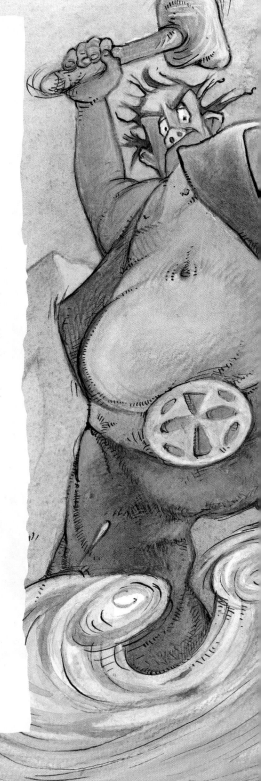

Once, there lived a man called Finn MacCool. He was a giant of a man – but a good giant! He lived in the north of Ireland and he led an army of warriors. Together, they protected Ireland from attack. And when they weren't fighting for the honour and safety of Ireland, they honed their skills by hunting deer and other wild animals.

Now, word reached Finn MacCool that over the water in Scotland there was another giant, named Benandonner, and Benandonner was laughing at Finn MacCool, mocking him, saying he wasn't really a giant and that he, Benandonner, had more strength in the middle finger of his right hand than Finn MacCool had in his whole body.

At this, Finn MacCool saw orange ... then red ... then his anger boiled over. In his rage, he scribbled a challenge to Benandonner, took a great handful of earth and rocks, tied his note to the biggest rock and hurled it across the water to Benandonner.

Not long after, a mighty rock came flying back across the water. It had Benandonner's reply attached to it.

TO FINN MACCOOL, THE SO-CALLED GIANT.
OF COURSE I COULD BEAT YOU IN A FIGHT.
YOU'RE NOT NEARLY AS BIG AS ME!
I HAVE MORE STRENGTH THAN YOU IN THE
MIDDLE FINGER OF MY RIGHT HAND!
I CAN'T SWIM OR ELSE I'D BE THERE TO
FIGHT YOU.
YOU STAY NICE AND SAFE ON YOUR SIDE OF
THE WATER AND THEN YOU'LL NEVER KNOW
HOW WEAK YOU ARE COMPARED TO ME!!
BENANDONNER – A REAL GIANT OF A MAN!

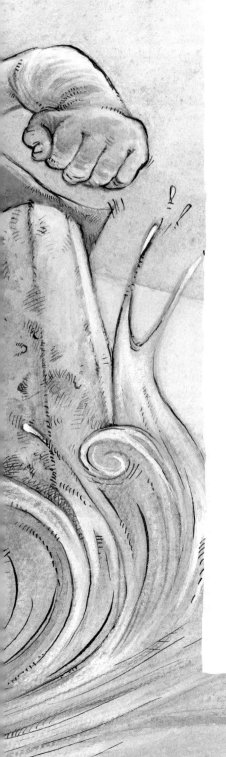

At this, Finn MacCool saw orange ... then red ... then his anger boiled over. He stormed to the coast of Ireland, picked up great pieces of volcanic rock that lay at the edge of the sea, and drove them, upright, into the sea bed. His fury lasted until he had pounded a causeway of pillars into the floor of the sea, stretching from Ireland all the way across to Scotland. He stood on Scotland's coast and yelled his challenge again to Benandonner, then he returned home across his newly built causeway.

The next day, Finn MacCool was in his house, having a cup of tea, when a neighbour burst through the door shouting, 'Finn MacCool! Finn MacCool! The biggest man I ever saw is coming here. We can see him crossing your new causeway. And he's a giant of a man. A real GIANT of a man.' To the neighbour's surprise, Finn MacCool calmly continued drinking his cup of tea.

Soon, another neighbour burst through the door shouting, 'Finn MacCool! Finn MacCool! The biggest man I ever saw is coming here. He has nearly crossed your new causeway. And he's a giant of a man. A real GIANT of a man.' To the second neighbour's surprise, Finn McCool continued calmly drinking his cup of tea.

Minutes later, a third neighbour burst through the door shouting, 'Finn MacCool! Finn MacCool! The biggest man I ever saw is coming here. He has crossed your new causeway. And he's a giant of a man. A real GIANT of a man.'

At this, Finn MacCool winked at his neighbours, crossed to his baby's cradle, squeezed himself inside, fastened his baby's bonnet on his own bristly head and pulled up the blankets. Just as he put his thumb into his mouth, the door crashed open on its hinges and the biggest man Finn MacCool had ever seen marched into his kitchen. Finn MacCool was so surprised at the size of the man that he nearly bit his own thumb off.

'Where is he?' stormed the giant. 'Where's Finn MacCool? I've come to show him that I've got more strength in the middle finger of my right hand than he has in his whole body!'

'He ... he's not here,' stammered one of the neighbours.

'He ... he had to go out,' stuttered another.

'But please be quiet, or you'll wake his baby,' whispered the third.

Benandonner looked at the cradle in the corner. 'Och, what a bonny wee baby!' he crooned. He reached in with the middle finger of his right hand to tickle the 'baby' under the chin. But Finn MacCool opened his mouth, removed his own thumb and caught Benandonner's finger between his teeth, crunching it with all his might. Benandonner's scream could be heard all the way back in Scotland. 'If that's the baby,' he roared, 'I'm not hanging around to meet the dad!' And he fled.

Benandonner ran. He ran back to Scotland without stopping once. And in his haste, he trod most of the pillars of the Giant's Causeway deep, deep beneath the waves. Finn MacCool and his neighbours stood on the coast of Ireland and laughed and laughed. As Benandonner approached Scotland, Finn MacCool pulled another piece of rock from the shore and flung it after the fleeing giant. But Finn MacCool was weakened with laughter and this piece of rock missed Benandonner and landed in the middle of the Irish Sea.

That piece of rock is now known as the Isle of Man. The hole left in the ground when Finn MacCool hurled his first challenge at Benandonner soon filled with water, and is now known as Lough Neagh – the largest lake in Ireland. And if you go to the north coast of Ireland, you will still see the remains of the Giant's Causeway. Some so-called 'experts' will have you believe that the causeway is really just columns of basalt which crystallised when lava was suddenly cooled in the sea – but now, you know better!

retold by Kate Ruttle

Balmoral Castle, Aberdeenshire,

The Balmoral Castle that we see today was built by Prince Albert for Queen Victoria.

In 1848, the royal couple rented the original Balmoral Castle, a 16th-century tower-house, and fell in love with the nearby countryside. In 1852, Albert bought the castle and the surrounding land – Balmoral Estate.

As the royal family grew (Victoria and Albert had nine children in all, as well as many servants), they needed more space at Balmoral. Prince Albert, with the help of a Scottish architect, designed a new castle at Balmoral that would be able to sleep 100 people comfortably. The style of architecture of the new castle, with its crenellations, turrets and towers, is called 'Scottish Baronial'.

The new Balmoral Castle was built in 1853–1856, 100 m from the original castle, which was pulled down.

Bertie at Balmoral, (aged 10, 1850)

Queen Victoria's second child, the Prince of Wales, Prince Albert Edward (Bertie), never made his own bed, cooked a meal or swept a floor. He had a manservant to dress him and tutors to teach him.
But Bertie's childhood was not an easy one. Queen Victoria and Prince Albert were very strict. Queen Victoria was disappointed in Bertie from an early age. While she was at Balmoral, Victoria went to visit families on the estate and performed royal duties. But she rarely took her eldest son with her to learn about being a monarch because she did not feel he was able to be taught to be the next king.

Staying at Balmoral Castle was no holiday for Bertie – his tutors came with him. He had to study for at least six hours a day, six days a week. As well as his standard studies, which included an hour each of French and German every day, Bertie had local nature studies too – learning about the plants and wildlife. Prince Albert took his older children onto the moors for wildlife study walks. He liked to fire questions at them and was very disappointed if they got anything wrong.

Although Bertie's tutors said he had a good memory and a sense of right and wrong, it was not enough for his parents. Bertie was pushed very hard, and sometimes he couldn't cope. He had terrible tantrums, throwing everything he could lay his hands on at the walls or windows. Sometimes, he would stand in a corner screaming.

The pastimes at Balmoral included hunting and fishing. Prince Albert and his guests hunted deer and game birds, but Bertie had to wait until he was a teenager before he could join the hunt. The one thing Bertie did turn out to be good at was fishing. At ten years old he was taught to fish for salmon by a gillie (gamekeeper) called John Grant. But even this did not please his mother. She was jealous of his skill.

The gillie s lad (aged 10, Balmoral, 1850)

I work as a gillie's lad on the Balmoral Estate. Gillies is what we call gamekeepers up here, and I'm a helper. I live with my family in a wee cottage on the estate.

The royal family are going to set up a school here, but I didn't get much schooling. Even when I did, I'd work after school. There's always something to be done. The estate has potatoes to lift, cabbages to cut, birds to scare, geese to tend, eggs to find ... you name it, it has to be done.

The job varies through the year. Over winter, we plant food crops for the grouse and partridge – the game birds. We feed the young birds in spring, to fatten them up. We manage the woods for the pheasants and deer – the trees have to be close enough together to make them feel safe, but not so close that we can't get in there.

All year round, we have to keep a lookout for poachers. They come for the rabbits, the salmon, the deer, the birds – anything.

I have to help at bird shoots and follow deer hunts and bring the prizes home. On one hunt they shot 300 deer in one day! That was a slaughter.

Prince Albert's a poor shot. He got two deer on a hunt the other day, but killed neither. They ran off into the woods. He didn't care a jot what happened to them, but I had to spend all night searching in the sodden rain for them.

Jeannie (aged 10), jute mill worker, Dundee, 1850

At the same time that Prince Bertie was living a privileged life in Balmoral Castle, other children in Scotland were living very different lives.

Jeannie worked 18 hours a day. The heat, the dust of the jute fibres, and the oil fumes from the machines could give you mill fever. Jeannie coughed a lot, and she went deaf from the noise of the machines.

Jeannie shared a box bed with three other mill girls in a crowded tenement (a block of flats). She was lucky, she said – some of the girls at work were sold to the mill owners and were kept under lock and key all the time.

One of the reasons mill owners employed children (apart from being able to pay them almost nothing!) was that they could put the machines closer together, because the children were so small. Once, Jeannie was working on a carding machine (a machine that 'combs' the jute fibres before they're spun into cloth) with her bed mate, Morag. Morag was so tired and hot that she fell asleep on her feet. She fell forward and her hair got caught around the teeth of the carding roller. Before anyone could help, Morag got drawn into the machine. She was dead before they could get her out. Jeannie joked that she had more room in the bed for a few days, but you could see the pain in her eyes.

Jute is a plant fibre which is woven to make rough fabric for things like tents, sacks and sails.

Extract from *The Body Snatcher*
by *Robert Louis Stevenson*

Robert Louis Stevenson is a famous Victorian writer whose works include *Treasure Island*. Some of his stories are set in his native Scotland, inspired by the criminals he met while studying law.

The story so far: Macfarlane and Fettes are two Edinburgh medical students. They get extra money by digging up corpses and selling them to the medical school to be cut up by students in their lessons. This excerpt is set in the dead of night. The pair have dug up the just-buried corpse of a farmer's wife. They have wrapped it in sackcloth, put it into their gig (horse-drawn carriage) and are taking it back to Edinburgh ...

They had both been wetted to the skin during their operations, and now, as the gig jumped among the deep ruts, the thing that stood propped between them fell now upon the one and now upon the other. At every repetition of the horrid contact each instinctively repelled it with the greater haste; and the process, natural although it was, began to tell upon the nerves of the companions. Macfarlane made some ill-favoured jest about the farmer's wife, but it came hollowly from his lips, and was allowed to drop in silence. Still their unnatural burden bumped from side to side, and now the head would be laid, as if in confidence, upon their shoulders, and now the drenching sackcloth would flap icily about their faces. A creeping chill began to possess the soul of Fettes.

Dover Castle, Kent, England

Dover has everything you could want in a castle. You can walk from a Roman lighthouse to a Second World War room all inside its walls.

The famous white cliffs of Dover are the UK's closest point to continental Europe, so in many wars, this fortress has been the UK's first line of defence against attack from abroad.

Strategic position – one cliffs, facing the enemy

Great Tower – a huge 29 m-cube
◆ walls – 6.4 m thick at bottom, 5.2 m at top
◆ well in tower goes 73 m into cliffs

Saxon church

On a hill

Inner curtain wall gives another line of defence

Roman lighthouse

Entrance to Second World War tunnels

Heavily defended main gate

Large bailey protected by outer curtain wall

Dover's first real castle was a motte and bailey put up in eight days by William the Conqueror, just after he won the Battle of Hastings.

Over time, the castle has been rebuilt and modernised. Most of the building work took place in medieval times, when a series of concentric circle walls were built. The idea was that if the outer wall was broken by an enemy, you could retreat behind the inner wall, making it more difficult for an attacker to capture the castle.

Dover Castle has seen its share of battles and sieges ever since Julius Caesar's time. It still played an important part in the Second World War.

Dover Castle in the Second World War (1939–1945)

In Dover Castle during the Second World War, heavy guns pointed out to sea. A system of tunnels, dug by medieval soldiers to launch surprise attacks, was expanded. By the end of the war, the tunnels occupied three levels and were used as a safe place from which to direct south-east England's coastal defences. Built into the tunnels were an underground hospital, barracks, telephone exchanges and operations rooms. The evacuation of Dunkirk was organised from here.

Castle glossary

bailey	courtyard
crenellations	cuts in the upper part of a parapet that let soldiers fire arrows more easily
curtain wall	wall going round a bailey (courtyard)
keep	the main tower
motte	a mound of earth
parapet	a low wall at the edge of a roof or earth mound, etc.
strategy	the planning of a war

Index

Unit 1
Uncle Bertie's Wacky Survival Manual

black mamba 13
crocodile 10
elephant 5
hippopotamus 9
lion 6, 7, 8
prey 6, 10, 11
rhinoceros 14, 15
savannah 6
scorpion 11
snake 13
venom 11, 13

Unit 2
Earth Speaking: My Life – Some Highlights

Africa 25, 29
animals 19, 27, 28–29, 30–31, 32, 33
Antarctica 29
Asia 18, 19, 25, 32
Australia 19, 29, 32
Bali 18, 19, 32
Big Bang 20, 21
continent 26, 28, 29, 33
crust 21, 24, 33
earthquakes 24, 25
evolution 27, 28–29, 30–31, 33
fossils 27, 29, 33
islands 18, 19, 30–31, 32
Lombok 18, 19, 32
magma 22, 23, 24, 33
mammals 27, 28–29, 33
marsupials 28–29, 33
mountains 24, 25, 33
North America 29
oceans 21, 24, 25
Pangaea 26, 27, 28
plants 27, 31, 33
South America 25, 29
Sun 20, 21
tectonic plates 22, 23, 24, 25, 26, 32, 33
volcanoes 21, 24, 27, 33

Unit 3
The Century of the Car

air bags 35, 39
amphibious cars 45
armoured cars 37
Armstrong, Neil 44
computers 34, 42–43, 46, 47
engine 36, 37, 38, 43, 44
factories 36, 42, 43
First World War 34, 36, 37
Ford 34, 42
fuel 38, 39, 47
Grand Prix 35, 40
jeeps 37
moon buggy 35, 44
robots 43
safety 38–39, 43, 47
Schumacher, Michael 35, 40
seat belts 39
Second World War 34, 36
speed 34, 38, 40–41, 45, 47
speed limits 40
speed records 41
tanks 36, 37
Thrust SSC 41
USA 35, 36, 37, 40, 42

Unit 4
Here Comes the Sun

Aborigine 55–58
Apollo 59–61
Australia 55–58
Canada 50–54
crows 50–54
fables 50
gods 50, 59–61
Greece 59–61
Hiawatha 62–63
Inuit 50–54
kookaburras 55–58
moon 55, 61
myths 50, 55, 59
Romans 59
stars 50, 51
Venus 55

Unit 5
Travel Trivia

Africa 66–67, 72–73
Algeria 64, 66–67
animals 67, 69, 72, 77
Asia 70–71, 76–77
Augustine of Hippo, St 67
buildings 67, 68
caves 67, 72
cities 67, 69, 70, 71,
   74–75, 77
desert 66, 67
earthquakes 66, 69, 71, 76
Europe 74–75, 76–77
Guatemala 64, 68–69
Japan 65, 70–71
lakes 72, 77
Lenin 77
Madagascar 65, 72–73
Mayans 68, 69
Monaco 64, 74–75
rainforest 69, 72
Romans 67
Russia 65, 76–77
Second World War 71
temples 67, 69
volcanoes 68, 69, 71, 76, 77

Unit 6
A Kingdom of Castles

Albert, Prince 87, 88, 89
Arthur, King 80–81
Balmoral Castle 87–89,
   90, 91
Bertie, Prince 87–88,
   90, 91
Cardiff Castle 79
crenellations 79, 87, 93
curtain wall 92, 93
Dover Castle 92–93
Dunluce Castle 82–83
England 80, 92–93
Giant's Causeway 83, 84–86
Ireland 82–83, 84–86
keep 79, 93
MacDonnell, Sorley Boy
   82, 83
Malory, Thomas 80
motte and bailey castles
   78–79, 92–93
parapet 79, 93
Romans 79, 92
Saxons 80, 92
Scotland 84–86, 87–91
Second World War 92, 93
Stevenson, Robert Louis 91
Victorians 79, 87–91
Victoria, Queen 87
Wales 79, 80
William the Conqueror 93